THE WORKING MEN'S
COLLEGE

AVSPICIVM   MELIORIS

ÆVI: MDCCCLIV.

James Bequest

R.E.TYLER DEL.   1913.   C.H.PERRY SC.

BOSTON
Tattershall & Croyland

THE CHURCH OF S. BOTOLPH

BOSTON
Tattershall & Croyland

By M. R. Lambert, M.A.
and R. Walker, M.A.

Oxford : Basil Blackwell
1930

Made and Printed in Great Britain at the KEMP HALL PRESS LIMITED
in the City of Oxford

AUTHORS' NOTE

THE aim of the Authors has been to provide the visitor to Boston with a book which will help him to recapture the spirit of past ages, and see not merely relics and memorials of those ages, but the pious zeal, the romance of commerce, the struggle against the forces of nature of which they are the living tokens.

The Authors have made full use of the documents, records and manuscripts in the Library at Boston and in the Bodleian Library, Oxford. They are also indebted for much inspiration and help from various books on the Fenland district by Pishey Thompson, W. H. Wheeler and G. Jebb, and from the *Victoria County History*.

Their thanks are due to Mr. H. E. H. Franklin, M.A., of Pembroke College, Oxford, for reading the manuscript and giving valuable criticisms and suggestions.

PREFACE

I AM pleased to accede to a request on the part of the Authors to write a preface for this book, for I have read it carefully and found it very interesting.

There is no doubt that the district with which it deals is a particularly interesting part of England and I hope that this book may help to make it better known and better appreciated. The Marshland Churches of the district are of course famous for their grandeur and dignity amongst students of mediæval architecture all over Western Europe—as well as naturally in America, a visit to this district being one of the favourite pilgrimages made by visitors from America, on account of its associations with the Pilgrim Fathers. This book comes at a happy moment in view of the Ter-centenary Celebrations in Boston, Massachusetts, U.S.A.

I think the book is written in a lively and interesting style and that it will doubtless prove of great interest to a large public, both here and in America.

Although a native of this district, I never tire of its great beauty in certain respects—particularly of the gorgeous sunsets which frequently occur over an enormous extent of sky, and the feeling of openness and expanse which the district conveys in such a marked manner. As one of the Authors suggests, this feeling of openness appears to be reflected in the character of many of the inhabitants. The romance of the old monastic towns of the locality has also always greatly appealed to me, as well as the interesting plants and wild life which abound in the district.

Although I have visited it many times, I never cease to marvel and wonder each time at the grandeur of the wonderful tower of Boston Church rising vertically on the meandering banks of the River Witham. I consider that it is certainly one of the architectural wonders of the world and it never fails to impress me profoundly. If only it were in Italy or on a river in one of the old German towns in the Rhineland, or in South Germany, certain people would think far more of it, and would go hundreds of miles to see it. However, people with a sense of taste or judgment of their own can appreciate the things we have at home without their having to be situated in foreign climes. If this book serves to make the beauties of this district better known, it will have served a useful purpose. I wish the book every success.

E. PICKWORTH FARROW.

Limehurst
    Spalding.
March, 1930.

CONTENTS

ILLUSTRATIONS

INTRODUCTION

'They have a beauty of their own these great Fens,
even now when they are dyked and drained, tilled and
fenced—a beauty as of the sea, of boundless expanse and
freedom. Overhead the arch of heaven spreads more
ample than elsewhere as over the open sea; and that
vastness gave, and still gives, such cloudlands, such
sunrises, such sunsets, as can be seen nowhere else
within these isles.'

C. KINGSLEY.

IN the heart of these low-lying Fens stands the once
famous old town of Boston, surrounded by the lowest
lands and marshes in the County of Lincoln. The
river Witham flows through the town on its way to
empty its waters into the Wash five miles distant; thus
Boston is built on both sides of that river which was its
ancient highway. Formerly this district was little
better than a watery morass, frequently inundated by
river and tidal floods, and served mainly as a feeding
ground for geese and wild fowl.

The Fenland is an extensive tract of low, level country
forming part of the great eastern plain of England. It is
limited on the north by the Wolds of Lincolnshire, and
stretches southward for a distance of sixty miles, having
an average elevation of five and a half feet below the
level of high water of spring tides. Thus this region
presents a wide expanse of unbroken flatness.

In former times much of this lay permanently under
water, and in these days it is difficult to realize the

dismal aspect presented by this level Fen, 'a prospect wild and wide,' and to picture the habits and surroundings of the ancient Fenmen who gained much of their livelihood by sailing over the broad waters in their canoes, fishing for pike and eels or snaring or shooting wild fowl, who built their huts on the swampy islands, and who often baffled their enemies by taking refuge among the tall reeds in the stagnant waters. Even in these conditions, for the old chroniclers it had its charms, nor to the monks was it a gloomy swamp, for to them—

> 'The bright mere gleamed like a mirror
> In the mid-day sun,'

and the sweep of the wide plain was itself 'a beauty as of the sea,' while William of Malmesbury speaks of it as 'a heaven for the delight and beauty thereof.'

Yet even to-day, a general impression prevails among those who do not know this district that it is a dreary land, intersected by long wide dykes, and crossed by raised straight roads, presenting nothing but bleak and monotonous scenery. On the contrary, it possesses many interesting, unique and attractive features.

Geographically, the Fens present a distinctive natural region in these islands. The rich grazing, potato, and corn lands are unrivalled for their fertility, whilst the general intelligence, physique, and health of the Fenfolk compare very favourably indeed with those of the inhabitants of any other part of the British Isles. Moreover, there is documentary evidence proving the great age to which some of the inhabitants live, thus showing that the district is exceptionally healthy. Although the Fens lack the variety of scenery offered by hill and dale, Nature has provided compensations. The atmosphere generally is fresh and bracing, for a day's fog is now

THE INTERIOR OF THE CHURCH OF S. BOTOLPH

very rare, and the people enjoy 'as sunny skies as beautiful starlit nights,' and magnificent distant landscapes as those in other parts of England, whilst the renowned sunsets over this low-lying country frequently present a picture of almost indescribable beauty. Further, this district being part of the eastern coastland, has a very low rainfall, and floods and inundations which formerly taxed all the powers and skill of engineers are now almost unknown since the drainage system is so thoroughly efficient. The old Cardyke and Fossway, first constructed by the Romans, still form part of the drainage system, whilst the Roman banks built along the coast, also serve their purpose by preventing the inroads of the sea.

Within this district, too, occurred social and political events important in history; and far-famed institutions of a bygone age, that have flourished and decayed, have left their numerous traces. Parish churches renowned for their size or beauty or historical associations, stand out as memorials of the faith of the ancient Fenmen; while the magnificent tower of S. Botolph's, Boston, rises high above the plain, and with its beacon lantern, seen from land and sea for forty miles around, stands like a guardian over the Fenlands.

A journey through the Fens in early autumn will convince the traveller of their unparalleled fertility, for the roads and the wide drains are bounded on either side by rich fields of corn and rarer crops such as flax, poppies, woad and peppermint; and stretching far away on the horizon are green pastures where graze cattle and sheep in the best of condition. Such an expanse of luxuriant nature from which rise the towers of numerous churches, and the characteristic windmills, is unique in these islands, and the whole aspect justifies the remark that 'Everything taken together, there are more good things than man could have the conscience to ask of God.' Although here and there patches of the old Fenland scenery remain, determination, ingenuity, and capital have transformed the Great Fen from a land of swamps and meres to the fertile prairie lands of England.

CHAPTER I

THE NEIGHBOURHOOD

PERHAPS the ancient town and port of Boston owes much of its mediæval fame and present importance to its geographical position, for it is situated on the east coast of England opposite the Low Countries of the Continent. It stands, too, at the mouth of the navigable river Witham, which, after following a circuitous course for 89 miles, empties itself into the Boston Deeps—a narrow channel of the Wash running parallel with the coast for about 15 miles.

The town is a municipal borough in the Parliamentary County of Holland-with-Boston in the S.E. of Lincolnshire, and is 34 miles from Lincoln City, 107½ miles from London by rail and 116 by road. At the last census the population was 16,100.

The surrounding low, flat region, now called Holland, has a level below that of high tides, though Boston itself stands 11 feet above sea level. A glance at the map will show that this low country is bounded on the west by the Lincoln Heights; thus, being sheltered from the rain-bearing winds, it has a low annual rainfall of about 24 inches. It therefore holds one of the driest positions in the British Isles, which is a great advantage, for nearly all the precipitation in this district has to be disposed of by artificial means. Meteorological records show, too, that the least rain falls during the first five months, and this, with the large amount of sunshine, is very favourable for agriculture.

Old writings on the Fenland, however, describe this
region as 'swampy, foggy and unhealthy,' and doubtless
such were the conditions before the drainage was
improved, when heavy fogs so frequently prevailed
throughout the day, and the inhabitants who lived on
the oozy mounds surrounded by stagnant swamps fell
early victims to rheumatism and ague. At the present
time a day's fog rarely occurs, for the efficient drainage
system and consequent higher temperature of the soil by
solar influence, has produced a clear and dry atmosphere,
so that the people, as a rule, enjoy excellent health and
live to a very old age. Formerly the death rate was very
high, but now it is quite common to meet persons of
more than four score years living an active life and in
full possession of their faculties. While the climate is
considered neither enervating nor depressing, yet the
environment of this low plain providing long distant
views, has had its effect upon the people, who, hard-
working and hospitable, lack that characteristic of
suspicion and distrust which one often finds among
dwellers of hills and dales. Here, too, there prevails a
general feeling of sturdy independence and content-
ment; and an absence of restlessness and love of change,
which one often associates with the more stimulating
air of higher altitudes. Nature, also, is very generous
and gives great returns for their hard work and perseverance, for the soil is of such high fertility that it
yields harvests of corn, potatoes and rarer crops which
are unequalled in any other part of these islands.

But the work of rescuing this land from its former
temporary or permanently flooded state, and providing
the present productive conditions, taxed for centuries
all the powers of the best engineers; for, from the few
scattered remarks of the Roman writers, we gather that

the Fenland, from the Trent to Huntingdon, was at that time one vast morass, into which the rivers of the Wash discharged their waters, and which was subject to constant inundations by the sea. These floods brought deposits of alluvial matter, so that long creeks were formed which afterwards became pools of stagnant water. Old writings show, too, that the scattered inhabitants dwelt in huts on the patches of high ground which were interspersed among the pools, their only means of communication in winter being wicker boats covered with skins.

During the Roman occupation great improvements were made by the building of high banks along the coast to prevent the inroads of the sea, and by the establishment of a system of artificial drainage. The Romans also opened a new channel for the Witham from Lincoln to Chapel Hill to provide a passage for boats, and by cutting the Fossdyke, a free communication was made between the Witham and the Trent. The former river then became the chief waterway for vessels engaged in exporting corn and importing wine, and Lincoln, which was a miniature Rome, became one of the most important centres of Roman Britain. The site of Boston, however, was at this time a vast salt marsh surrounded by a huge morass, and ill-suited for the foundation of an ancient city.

The early inhabitants of this district, called the Iceni, were taught by the Romans to grow corn; and the fertile lands bordering the Fens were brought under tillage, making this country the most profitable province in the Roman Empire.

Although these people sought alliance with the Romans and submitted to the Roman power, they still adhered to their own mode of living among their forests and marshes, and cherished their original spirit of independence. Yet they were forced to furnish the manual labour for the drainage work, and it is recorded that they complained that the Romans wore out their bodies in embanking the Fens. These banks, however, afforded a security for the natives who waded up to their middle in water and dwelt in the huts on the oozy islands; they also provided a camp of refuge for the inhabitants against all invaders, for it was difficult for any military force to dislodge them. Nevertheless, after the Roman evacuation, this district became an easy prey to the Saxons, and very soon all traces of the early Britons disappeared. Then the newcomers in their turn held their own against all succeeding invaders, so that the Fenland in names and manners is perhaps more purely Saxon than any other part of England.

The new settlers brought with them the art of agriculture, and soon began producing wheat for bread and barley for beer. No further drainage improvements, however, were made until the introduction of Christianity, when this district became the refuge of saints and monks: among these was S. Botolph, the founder of the monastery of Boston. Owing to the abundance of fish in the waters, many other monasteries were established along the Witham; and records show that the Abbots became the prime movers in all works of reclamation. The land was then used for tillage and pasturage, the wood and turf were used as fuel, the reeds for thatching, and the fish and the water fowl were caught for food. This growing prosperity, however, was checked by the constant incursions of the Danes, who, under Sweyn, finally pillaged and destroyed all the monasteries, S. Botolph's being among them.

During the Norman invasion, the Fens again became

the refuge for Saxons from all parts of the country; and
when all the rest of England was subdued, the Fenmen
still refused allegiance, for their isolation and solitary
habits had made them tenacious of their ancient rights
and loyal to their masters. They put up a bold fight
for liberty, and finally, instead of the Fenmen accepting
the manners and language of the Normans, the Normans
gradually became converted into Fenmen.

After the Norman Conquest, however, this region
again became a colony of monks. The Abbots, who
were the chief landowners, soon set to work to drain
the marshes and clear the woods, and so converted the
country along the Witham into rich and profitable
lands. Communication along the river, too, had
increased, and so Boston was rapidly becoming an
important trading centre and port.

Various effective drainage schemes were carried out.
In 1142 the navigation of the lower Witham had become
obstructed by deposits of mud, so the first great sluice
was erected at Boston to allow the water drained from
the land to flow out more easily and clear away the
debris. As a result of the improvements made during
these early years, Boston, by the thirteenth century, not
only carried on a large home trade, but so much business
was transacted with the Netherlands and other countries
of the Continent, that the town and port rose to the very
first rank. Owing to the accumulation of mud in the
Witham, moreover, navigation to Lincoln had become
impossible, so that in 1369, the Staple for wool was
transferred from Lincoln to Boston.

Frequent floods, however, caused great misery in the
district, and in 1287 a high tide and violent storm
destroyed a great part of Boston, with much loss of
life, for at that time the duty of repairing banks and

drains rested upon private owners who often neglected it. As a result of other serious floods in 1335, 1439 and 1467, continual complaints were made to the Crown. These led, in 1543, to the issue of various Commissions to provide for the security of the Fenlands, and this arrangement lasted until the reign of Henry VIII, when an Act was passed which constitutes the origin of the Court of Sewers. Several efforts were made by this body to render the drainage secure, among them being the cutting of the Maud Foster drain in 1586. As the Court was unable to enforce necessary taxes, however, no really effective schemes were established. More serious floods frequently burst the embankments. That of 1571 provided the subject of a poem by Jean Ingelow; and in 1625, the highest tide ever known brought great desolation. A result of this was the starting of a new enterprise; for in 1631, the management of the drainage was taken over by a number of adventurers who undertook to carry out the necessary construction of banks, drains and sluices in return for grants of reclaimed land. This scheme worked successfully; and for seven years they enjoyed the fruits of their labour, until the jealous and dispossessed Fenmen attacked the adventurers and completely destroyed their works. Thus both the Crown and adventurers failed utterly to rescue these drowned lands. The region then reverted to its original conditions and so remained for nearly another century.

These conditions were very miserable, for previous to the final reclamation of the Fenland at the end of the eighteenth century, Dugdale describes this district as 'having no element good.' It consisted then of marshes and fens, the former being rich alluvial land but poorly drained, and the latter, interspersed among the marshes, forming extensive tracks of low, peaty land with large meres and permanent pools of water through the winter.

On the raised mounds lived the Fenmen who attended to their cattle on the fens and marshes, which provided valuable grazing in summer; and on the higher lands adjacent to the Fens were the villages with their fine Norman churches. Here the conditions of the inhabitants and their means of communication with the rest of the world, were neither better nor worse than in any other part of England. Down on the Fens, however, conditions were very wretched, for on the isolated patches among the meres lived the Fen Sloggers, as they were called, who were bitterly opposed to any system of drainage. These 'half-amphibious beings,' as Macaulay described them, lived in their wooden huts erected on the isolated oozy mounds among the chain of meres surrounded by dense crops of reeds, and communicated with each other by means of crude canoes, or mounted on stilts, and gained their living by fishing and shooting or snaring wild fowl. Though they were miserable victims of ague, and at an early age became permanently bent and twisted with rheumatism, yet they enjoyed their wild liberty, for the Fen was their native land. The flood was their harvest, for the water brought fish, and the fish attracted wild fowl which they could snare or shoot. For this reason, they met the reclaimers everywhere with wild opposition, and frequently destroyed the drains and banks which were being constructed, thus making it necessary for the work to be done under armed protection.

Their cause was not without sympathizers, and, moreover, was supported by learned men of the day: for Fuller, the historian, suggests that probably 'Providence had specially left this district for the production of fish, fowl, turf, and reeds.' Opposition to any drainage system also came from the owners of the higher lands, who saw that if the Fens were drained, he value of their lands would be depreciated. Yet their means of communicating with the Fens were often cut off, for the roads which ran from the high country to Boston, though outlined by willows, were so frequently under water that guides who moved about on stilts were engaged to conduct strangers across.

Thus the early history of the Fens tells of liberty and some measure of prosperity, and the systematic drainage remained for centuries a huge question beset with many difficulties; and caused long and bitter disputes. The Fenmen remained, however, in unchanged conditions till 1761, when an Act was passed providing for the improvement of the lands of the lower Witham. In 1764 the Witham was straightened and deepened, the Grand Sluice was built and other drainage schemes were put into operation. Later, at the beginning of the nineteenth century, the engineer, Rennie, reverted to the Roman system of drainage, by which the water from the artificial drains was conducted into the natural channels, contrary to the method adopted by the reclaimers of the Middle Ages, who made the natural drains subservient to the artificial, a method which was followed by great disaster.

The present system works by means of a number of canals and dykes into which the water is drained off the land. The main drains discharge their waters into the tidal rivers, which are protected from the tides by sluices with self-acting doors. These automatically close when the tidal water reaches a higher level than that of the water flowing down the drains, and open again when the tide recedes so that the drainage water may flow out. The land along the coast also is protected against the inflowing tides by high sea banks, but constant care has to be exerted over these banks, for the least neglect of the smallest breach may quickly turn the fields of corn into a sea of water. In the past much damage has frequently been caused by high tides which have flooded the streets and houses in Boston; and in 1807, the tide rose so high that the water flowed into the Church. Other high tides occurred in 1810, 1820, and 1883, when breaches in the sea banks brought disastrous results, with loss of life and property.

So in the end the reclamation of the Fens and their present prosperity are due to the ingenuity and perseverance of the inhabitants, aided by the skill of some of the most eminent engineers of the past century; which has resulted in a complete change in the geographic and economic conditions of this district.

CHAPTER II

THE NATURAL HISTORY

THE natural history of the Boston district is interesting, and its bird and animal life is in many respects unique. Geological observations testify that in remote times portions of this region were sites of extensive woods, but owing to climatic changes, the influence of man, and herds of domesticated animals, the luxuriant covering of these portions gradually disappeared, and this district became transformed into the treeless swamps of the dreary undrained Fens. No less remarkable has been the subsequent change, brought by artificial drainage, from the water-logged morasses to the rich cornfields.

These altered conditions have naturally had their effect on the fauna and flora, for in their wild state, the fens provided a suitable habitat for all varieties of marsh vegetation, and many unusual birds and insects.

In these early days, on the mounds flourished willows and alders in wild luxuriance, and on the swamps, with no common dominant, hydrophilous plants formed themselves into a number of small associations, over which often a single species predominated, according to the soil conditions, while the lakes and meres were dominated by reeds and sedges.

The drainage and high cultivation of this neighbourhood has necessarily wrought a vast destruction of this indigenous vegetation, so that many species which once were abundant have become rare; others formerly so common, linger on the very few patches of untilled fen, or in places where they have had to adapt themselves to their new and drier environment; while a few are probably extinct.

Though every possible square yard of land is now under cultivation, neglected ditches or ponds on the low peat land soon show a dense growth of reeds, sedges, and bullrushes, and ancient submerged plants abound among the clusters of water-lilies. On the higher silt lands, too, the ditches in summer become bright with water forget-me-not, valerian, iris, water purslane, and water buttercups, with other water plants which revel in their ancient luxuriance. Such scenes as these, however, still provide a glimpse of the quaint and picturesque character of the flora of the primitive fens.

Yet many of the bog plants, including the marsh violet (Viola stagnina), bog pimpernel (Anagallis tenella), and the bog myrtle (Myrica gale) have almost disappeared; the sedge (Cladium mariscus), which formerly provided large masses of herbage and was also used for lighting fires, is now a delicate lingerer; the beautiful white tufted cotton grass (Eriophorum angustifolium), once so abundant and conspicuous, now lingers only in a few places; and the water lily (Nymphæa alba), and the water marigold (Bidens cernua), once so plentiful, are not so common now; while the marsh fleawort (Cineraria palustris), marsh thistle (Sonchus palustris), and the fen ragwort (Senecio paludosus), formerly so abundant, are now extinct.

While several species of plants were peculiar to these Fens, perhaps this flora is made more remarkable by the absence of some of the generally common plants. The primrose (Primula vulgaris) and the sweet violet (Viola odorata), so common in most parts of the British Isles, are entirely absent, and the cowslip is found only on the higher silt lands.

Though this region has lost some of its native plants, many fresh species have been imported in consequence of the drier conditions or as a result of cultivation. The most remarkable immigrant is the submerged water plant (Anacharis alsinastrum) generally known as Thyme weed or American weed. This plant belongs to a species peculiar to North America, and was first discovered here in 1847, but by 1852 it had been so prolific, that numerous streams and sluices had been choked up by myriads of these individuals, which had thus impeded both drainage and navigation. Those plants which have come as a result of cultivation and drier conditions are the common whitlow-grass (Draba verna), the biting stone crop (Sedum acre), and many others now found on walls, and everywhere on very dry situations. others are found as corn weeds, perhaps the most familiar ones being the poppy and hemp nettle (Galeopsis versicolor).

Willows and alders still fringe the moister situations, though the oak, ash, beech, birch, and poplar, requiring drier soils, are now quite common on the silt and marsh lands. On the lower fens the insectivorous sundew and butterwort are still found, and the clubmoss, the marsh fern, the beautiful grass of Parnassus and the marsh gentian are all distinguished inhabitants. On the salt marsh, below the level of high water, appears the glasswrack, which is followed by a zone of glasswort, locally miscalled samphire. This is succeeded at higher levels by sea lavender, sea blite, sea purslane, and coarse grass, which then gives place to the more ordinary and varied species of plant life.

The vegetation of the whole region, however, is still

rich in species, for the district seems to provide a meeting ground for various plants which are usually found on differing soils and at different altitudes; but this unusual and cosmopolitan assembly may be due to the variety of soils and their changed conditions together with the absence of any mountain barrier.

The bird life of the region, too, is full of interest, for from earliest times it has been famous for the number and variety of wild fowl; and in its primitive condition, it formed a congenial home for these as well as other birds. For not only were the more common ones found here, such as the teal, woodcock, quail, and the now preserved pheasant and partridge, but knots, puits, godwits, and dotterells, and, as Camden says, 'such as have no Latin names.' These, he says were 'the delicacies of the table, the food of heroes, and fit for the palates of the Great' (Wheeler).

From earliest times this low peat shore has offered a most favourable feeding ground and habitat for the migratory fowl which visit our east coast in winter from over the North Sea; and this region, too, was the haunt of the ruff and reeve, wild duck, geese, black tern, cootes, redshanks, and many other water fowl which sheltered in the rushes, while the migratory birds inhabited the open spaces. Since the altered conditions of the Fens, various former residents have disappeared, while others remain only in smaller numbers.

The study of this former natural aviary shows that some of the birds were particularly choice, either as providing delicate meat, or from the beauty of their plumage. The knot, brought from Denmark by Canute, and the dotterell, are two birds of delicate meat, and formerly appeared in large numbers along the coast. The dotterells had also very attractive habits, and were extremely imitative, and so they were easily caught, for we are told these birds would imitate the fowler, 'That if he put out an arm, they raised a wing, and if he a leg, they did the same,' and soon the net was drawn over them. The ruffs and reeves, too, were famed for beautiful plumage, and the bittern, noted for its melancholy booming, heard for miles over the Fenlands, was also distinguished by its beauty.

The charm of this varied bird life has been felt by many great writers, such as Kingsley :

'By many a mere and many an ea; through narrow reaches of clear, brown glassy water; between the dark green alders, between the pale green reeds, where the coot clanked and the bittern boomed, and the sedge bird, not content with its own sweet song, mocked the song of all the birds around: and then out into the broad lagoons, where hung motionless, high over head, hawk beyond hawk, buzzard beyond buzzard, kite beyond kite, as far as the eye could see.'

Owing to the changed conditions, many of the aquatic birds have been driven from their old breeding haunts and songsters have occupied the land. The bustards, weighing up to 14 lbs., which were hunted by dogs since they could not rise quickly, have not been seen since 1855; the bittern, too, has vanished, the last being shot in 1848; the last kite's nest was taken in 1870; and several other species have not visited this region for many years.

Though many of these feathered creatures have been driven away by the drier conditions, the common wild duck seems to have increased since the Wild Birds' Protection Act of 1880. Cranes are still residents here, and among the wading birds there remain the curlew, lapwing, golden plover, green shank, redshank, reeve, and whooper; Berwick swans and several kinds of wild geese are welcome visitors here in hard weather. The knut, or knot, is still plentiful on the extensive mud banks, and the little dunlins, or stints as they are locally called, also flit along the shore in large flocks, and are caught in considerable numbers by flight netters of the district. The merlin appears only as a winter visitor, and the kestrel is seen but in lessening numbers, while the delightful ruff is now quite rare.

From this wealth of bird life, the ancient Fenmen gained most of their livelihood, for as many as 3,000 ducks could be taken at a drive, whilst the inhabitants of the higher country also found here a lucrative sport. Formerly herons were numerous here, and disused heronries still remain in the district. Large numbers of decoys, too, were used for snaring wild fowl. Decoy ducks trained for the purpose enticed the unwary birds from pools into small channels which were covered with nets. Large numbers were captured in this way, for we read that in one season ten decoys furnished 31,000 birds for the London markets.

In spite of the changed conditions and increased population, the wild duck gunners are still engaged in their trade along the flat marshes. A small open punt is generally used, fitted with a duck gun weighing about one and a half cwt., which will often bring down twenty or thirty birds at one shot. Large numbers of pheasants and partridges still make their homes on the arable land, and their enemies, the weasels and stoats, are quite common.

The natural history of this district would not be complete without reference to the inland fisheries which have had a recognized value from early times. Frequently rents were paid in fish which abounded in the creeks; and, owing to the abundance and quality, many religious houses were established along the banks of the Witham. The most plentiful fish were eels and pike; but the Witham appears to have been stocked with a variety of fresh water fish. A farm near Boston annually paid a rent of 1,500 eels, and the town of Croyland paid £300 yearly to the Abbot for permission to fish in the streams. Further, owing to the abundance of fish, we read that the Abbots' stew ponds were so plentifully supplied, 'that the Lents and fast days of the Abbeys had more the appearance of festivals than days of mortifications.'

The streams and drains, however, are still stocked with a large variety of fish, which yield great quantities of food and give much sport to anglers, who come in considerable numbers in summer from Sheffield and other large towns.

THE GUILDHALL, BOSTON

CHAPTER III

INDUSTRIES AND COMMERCE

FROM the earliest days Boston has been a centre of activity, both religious and industrial. The great founder, S. Botolph himself, must have been an indefatigable worker, since we are told that he and his monks toiled and prayed in a region full of dangers and difficulties, and yet he established the nucleus of a town destined to become the first port of the Kingdom.

At that time the surrounding region of marsh and mere offered little encouragement to its early settlers, and gave them only a supply of fish, fowl, reeds, and turf to support a comfortless life in their primitive dwellings.

Boston, however, was destined to benefit by the existence, a few miles inland, of the famous Roman city of Lincoln, already a centre of much business, trading particularly in corn, wool, and wine. These goods were conveyed along the river Witham, and as Boston was situated at the mouth of the same river and faced the Low Countries, it rapidly rose to a position of importance.

Still the earliest records relating to its commerce are not found until the reign of King John, when a tax, called the Quindene, was levied on all movable goods in the kingdom; for we read that in the year 1205 Boston paid the sum of £780 15s. 3d., and came second only to London, which paid £856. As yet England had not discovered her mineral resources or become a manufacturing country, so she produced only raw material,

17

chiefly wool, which was dyed in this country, then
exported to Flanders for manufacture, and afterwards
sent back to England.

Again Boston was favourably situated, for on the
rich pastures on the higher mounds of the Fens, and on
the hills to the west, thousands of sheep were reared.
Conditions in the neighbourhood, too, were improving,
and the Cistercian monks, who owned Revesby and
Swineshead Abbeys, quite near to Boston, were great
producers of and dealers in wool; in fact, they were
charged with 'being more like farmers than monks.'

At this period, too, the only internal communications
were the waterways and the Roman roads; so Boston
became the natural outlet for surplus produce from
about eighteen counties, since it was the port at the
mouth of the Witham, a river navigable as far as Lincoln,
and there connected by the Fossdyke to the Trent and
its numerous streams. All the trade of England was
eastward, and France, Holland, and Flanders were our
chief markets. Boston, therefore, increased as a port
and trading centre, and by 1259 foreign traders, known
as Hanseatic Merchants, or Merchants of the Steelyard,
had settled in the town. So much business was now
transacted, that the town soon became the residence of
numerous wealthy foreign merchants, who were protected by the Crown and conducted their business under
the direction of a Merchant Guild. The trade of the
town had so increased that the returns of the duties for
the next few years show that, by 1287, Boston had
risen to be the commercial capital, and paid now one
third more than London, and by good fortune, it
maintained this first position throughout the thirteenth
and fourteenth centuries. So great was the wool trade
here, that in 1297 Boston was made a Staple town for

this great native commodity. At this time all the trade
of the country moved in definite channels, so that the
Staple towns were those to which by authority and
privilege, wool, wine, hides, corn, and foreign merchandise were conveyed to be sold, and also places of deposit
for home produce for sale to foreign merchants. Thus,
under the Staple system, free trading was prohibited,
for the duties on these goods were levied by royal
officials at the Staple town, and so the royal revenue
was increased.

Again Boston was favourably situated to receive both
home and foreign goods. Business was carried on at the
Steelyard, where all the goods were weighed and stamped
by the Mayor of the Staple with the Staple Seal. The
Staple brought much wealth to the town, for not only
did ships come from Norway, Holland, France, and
Belgium, but many merchants from Calais and Cologne
resided in the town.

In those times there were no shops, or at any rate
very few, so that many of the necessities of life had to
be purchased at the annual fairs which were established
in many towns, and even by the thirteenth century the
Great Fair of S. Botolph's was famed not only throughout this country, but also on the Continent. Great
quantities of goods were brought to the fair, and people
visiting from far and near, furnished themselves with a
sufficiency of articles of every kind—especially clothing
—until the next fair. Many foreign traders came to the
fair, and it was attended by the greatest celebrities of
the homeland, for the Fair of S. Botolph was one of the
great events of the year. Old records show that in
1252 the King's butler bought 100 tuns of wine at the
fair, and in 1277 he again bought such large quantities
of wine that he rented cellars in Boston for its storage.

We read, too, that many religious Foundations annually replenished their stores at the fair, for the Canons of Bridlington regularly attended the fair, where they bought articles of dress of superior quality, 'such as could not be bought at home'; the Abbot of Melsa, three miles from Hull, and the Canons of Bolton Abbey came to make their purchases, and the monks of Bardney and other monasteries also imported their wine from the Elbe and Rhine via the port of Boston.

We read, moreover, that many of the wealthy traders were also inveterate smugglers; and on one occasion a fine of £1,000 was imposed on an offender by Henry III, for using false weights.

The town thus continued to be a wealthy commercial emporium until the close of the fourteenth century, when natural circumstances brought about its decline; for we see that its prosperity waned after the discovery of the Cape of Good Hope in 1486, and of the New World in 1492, when the movement of trade began to take a westward direction. Then followed the Dissolution of the Religious Houses and the Mercantile Guilds, and after Leland visited the town in 1530, he wrote 'The Staple and the Stiliard houses yet there remayne, but the stiliard is little or nothing at all occupied.' Later, however, the trade had so declined that foreign merchants left the town, and many Bostonians sought new homes abroad. The commercial depression continued, till by the seventeenth century Boston seems to have sunk so low that it was declared a 'decayed and ruined port,' and the position was so reduced that the Corporation petitioned Parliament to place their borough among the 'decayed towns.'

At the close of the last century, however, conditions in the immediate neighbourhood began to improve owing to the effective drainage operations in Holland and Wildmore Fens, and again the commerce of Boston began to revive. Immense quantities of grain passed through the market and port for shipment to London and other centres, for the surrounding district of marsh and fen was now transformed into the richest cornlands in the Kingdom.

To-day, Boston is still a busy, interesting, but small market town, holding its annual fairs in May and its markets on Wednesdays and Saturdays. It also has its own peculiar industries. Two large feather factories, established in the days when large flocks of geese were reared on the undrained fens, still maintain an old distinctive Lincolnshire industry. Though the demand for feathers generally is not as great as in former times, the industry is much encouraged locally among the Fenfolk, who enjoy the comfort, even though un-healthy, of their feather beds. Many people, too, find employment in the old-established rope factory, and in the cigar and whiting factories; while others are engaged in the several breweries, flour mills, and oil-cake mills. Pea-sorting and packing is a new and growing industry, and gives employment to a large number of women and girls. The numerous flour mills, which formerly were a distinctive feature of the landscape of this neighbourhood, are now rapidly disappearing. The old local industry of grinding corn by the village windmill has almost died out, and the flour for local use is now prepared by the mills at Boston.

The Port of Boston gives employment to many workers, for it is a natural outlet from the industrial centres to the Continent. As constituted in 1898, it extends north to Trusthorpe Drain, and on the south to Fleet Haven Outfall, so as to include both Spalding and Wainfleet. The trade of the port, which began to decline again about the middle of the last century owing to the accumulation of silt in the river bed, revived when the river was deepened and the docks reconstructed, and continued to increase until 1914. The port also claimed a considerable fishing industry which was carried on by the trawlers of the Deep Sea Fishing Company, and by the smaller craft engaged in Boston Deeps. The trading statistics show that 389 steam vessels entered the port in 1913, and the imports amounted to £1,000,000. These consisted of the following: barley (£90,000), maize (£100,000), refined sugar (£400,000), timber (£100,000), manures and general goods. The trade connections were mainly with the Baltic for timber, the Mediterranean for grain, cotton, and linseed, and with the Black Sea and America for other goods. In 1913, too, there were 98 fishing vessels engaged in deep sea fishing at Dogger Bank and off the shores of Iceland, landing fish to the value of upwards of £150,000.

The trade of the port was badly crippled by the Great War. In 1918 the imports amounted to £20,000, and the fishing ceased; but in 1920, though both trade and fishing had revived, they were much below pre-war standard, for only 300 vessels entered the port and 47 vessels were engaged in deep sea fishing.

It is perhaps interesting to note that the great fishing industry of our country had its origin at this port, a fact which is singularly appropriate to the town of S. Botolph, who is the saint of seafaring men. Records of the fourteenth century frequently refer to the great fish market at Boston. Later history tells us how Queen Elizabeth ordered the stricter observance of fast days, not on the ground of conscience, but because by so doing the fishing trade was increased, and as a result more men were engaged in seafaring, which was essential for England's safety during those ages. Consequently, the fishing industry here was encouraged, and continued to maintain its ancient reputation, for we read that offerings of the spoil of Boston Deeps were often sent to distinguished personages.

The chief industry of the surrounding district is agriculture, and much local produce supports the Wednesday and Saturday markets. Since the land here has been so extensively and scientifically drained, the soil yields the best possible results. The rich loam land around Boston is of such high fertility that every possible square yard is brought under cultivation and produces enormous harvests of wheat, potatoes, oats, beans, and peas. Perhaps wheat is the most extensive crop in this region, the dry climate and rich soil being admirably adapted to its cultivation, so much so that many harvests yield nine and ten quarters per acre, as compared with the average yield for England of four and a half quarters. Potatoes, too, are now very extensively grown, and the soil gives enormous returns. The yield varies according to the weather, but early crops produce 8–10 tons per acre, while the later varieties yield 10–16 tons under favourable conditions. Oats also give excellent results, the average yield being nine quarters per acre, which is eight bushels per acre over the average for the country. During recent years sugar beet has been successfully cultivated, and the produce of thousands of acres now supports the sugar refining factories at Spalding and Peterborough. This district, too, is noted for the production of unusual crops, some of which are unique, and others are not grown elsewhere in this country. Some of these special crops include mustard, celery, green vegetables, bulbous flowers, flax, beet, peppermint, poppies, and woad. Formerly peppermint was considerably grown; now only a small quantity is produced. Poppies were also extensively cultivated for the extraction of laudanum, which was the general remedy for ague, so prevalent in this area. Woad, used for a dye, was also grown on a large scale, but it is now confined to a small area of six acres about five miles from Boston. The world's supply is entirely restricted to this one field, for woad as a dye has been superseded by indigo. The process of growing and manufacture, however, is the same now as in the twelfth century. The seed is sown in March, and when the plant is eight inches high, the leaves are gathered and crushed in a mill with crude conical crushers, and the pulp is then allowed to ferment in water in a dark room.

Scattered about the district, too, in Spring, are fields of flowering daffodils, snowdrops, narcissi, and tulips, which are cultivated for Covent Garden. This loamy clay also produces rich pasture which is now better suited to horses and cattle than to sheep. The original Lincolnshire cattle were large-boned, coarse and hardy creatures, and the old Lincolnshire sheep has been described as an 'ungainly animal,' but the chief merit of the sheep was its wool which grew from twelve to eighteen inches long, and this heavy fleece was profitable.

Everywhere in this region nature rewards labour, and the Lincolnshire farmer fully realizes the value of cultivating his land on a scientific basis. Many large farmers have their soil chemically analyzed to ensure a suitable rotation of crops. The land is so highly cultivated that two or three crops are now grown simultaneously in the same field to mature at different times of the year. Celery, for instance, is planted between drills of potatoes, and when the potatoes are lifted, their ridges are planted with cauliflowers, or sown with spring cabbage; and a winter crop of turnips or mustard follows the celery, and so on.

These Fen farms usually range from 50 to 400 acres, but as the soil is so fertile, 20 acres will support a family very well. Before this region was effectively drained, the value of the land was about £3 per acre, but in 1919 the price ranged from £100 to £200 per acre. The rate of wages for the agricultural labourer here has always been higher than in other parts of England, consequently the workers are well fed, strong, healthy, and intelligent. The character of the landlord, too, is reflected in the tenants and their farms. The farm houses are commodious and solidly built; the labourers' houses and buildings are up to date and kept in good state of repair; and the farmyards, full of huge stacks of corn often stored till after Christmas, are themselves a witness to the prosperity of the countryside. In spite of the frequent agricultural depressions in this region, many fortunes have been made from potatoes and other crops during the past few years.

CHAPTER IV

HISTORICAL SKETCH OF BOSTON, LINCOLNSHIRE

'Let us now praise famous men, and our fathers that
begat us. There be of them that have left a name behind
them, that their praises might be reported. And some
there be which have no memorial.' Eccles. xliv.

ACROSS the mists of centuries many are the saints
and heroes whose memory is preserved for ever
in the names of towns and villages called after
them. Earls Algar, Leofric, and Wibert, once heroes of
Lincolnshire in its struggle against the Danes, could
have no more fitting memorial than the names Algarkirk,
Leverton, and Wiberton. So it is also with S. Botolph,
whose figure from the great tower or Stump of his
church stands as guardian over the little town called by
his name. Once Botolph's Town or Boston in Lincolnshire was great, then when its glory waned it was fitting
that its greatness should be revived in the sister-city of
Boston, U.S.A., in its beginning so intimately connected
with Botolph's Town—but this is later history.

S. Botolph himself was and is no mere local saint.
There are sixty-three churches in England and others
in Norway and Sweden dedicated to him, and the
Venerable Bede tells us that though he was English he
received his training in Germany, where he and his
brother Adolph took religious vows as monks. Adolph,
however, remained in Germany and eventually became
Bishop of Maestricht, while Botolph's heart drew him

back to his native land, and having obtained the permission and interest of Ethelmund, King of East Anglia, in 654, he 'began to build a minster at Icanho' in the same year that 'King Anna was slain' (*A. S. Chron.*), and here in 'a certain untilled place, where no man dwelt, a wilderness unfrequented by men,' deep in the fens beside the River Witham, S. Botolph and his monks prayed and worked, and here in 680 the saint died (Capgrave, *Vita Botolphi*).   His name, said to mean 'commanding wolf,' may give a clue to the character of the man and the saint.

When Lincolnshire fell a prey to the Danish invasions of 869–70, not a church or a religious house was left standing in a district which had been rich in both, but the bones of S. Botolph were conveyed away in safety, part to Ely and part to Thorney, and in the latter place the Saint found a biographer in Folcard, Abbot of Thorney.

At some time unknown S. Botolph's monastery was refounded, and when William the Conqueror granted the lands of the neighbourhood as part of the Honour of Richmond to his nephew, Alan Rufus (Son of Eudo, Earl of Brittany), he in his turn granted the patronage of the church to the Abbey of S. Mary at York, and the gift was confirmed by his brother and successor, Alan Niger, and by Henry II (Dugdale's *Monasticon*).

As a town there is no mention of Boston until 1113, when it is recorded by Ingulphus, the Chronicler of Croyland Abbey, that 'Fergus, a brazier of S. Botolph's town, gave to Croyland Abbey two skillets ' (probably bells) 'which supplied the loss of the bells and tower.' Croyland had been burnt down in 1091, and the gift of Fergus argues considerable prosperity in the town which had evidently been growing up round the monastery of S. Botolph, but which in 1085 had not been of sufficient importance to be separately recorded in Domesday Book, but had been lumped in with Skirbeck, for—

> Though Boston be a proud town
> Skirbeck compasseth it around.

For the next three hundred years Boston had reason to be a proud town. The disabilities of townsfolk in the Middle Ages were very galling, subject as they were to the lord of the manor with his rights and privileges, the King's sheriff, who having farmed the taxes made what he could out of the tax-payers, and the Clerk of the King's markets, who had many subtle ways of extracting money from the helpless townsfolk.

In the struggle for independence, which makes up so much of the history of mediæval towns, Boston seems to have been fortunate. As part of the Honour of Richmond it was possessed by a lord who had more than four hundred and fifty manors in different parts of the country, and who would not therefore concern himself very greatly about so small a corner of his domains, and thus it was that the town took the opportunity to obtain its first Charter from King John, for which the King was well paid, which was no doubt what he chiefly desired. 'The men of Boston, of the soke (jurisdiction) belonging to the Honour of Richmond in Holland, paid £100 and two palfreys that no sheriff or his bailiffs should interfere, or have anything to do with them: but that they might choose a bailiff from among themselves who should answer to the Exchequer for pleas and outgoings, as they were wont to answer to the Earl of Brittany while it was in his hands.' Thus they became at least nominally free from the interference of extraneous officers, and the jurisdiction of their

absentee lord, though the whole situation was com-
plicated at the times of the fairs, when it appears that
any lord who could press a claim for tolls or the jurisdiction of a court did so. Complete freedom does not
seem to have been obtained until the Honour lapsed
to the Crown, and granted by Edward III to his son
John, Duke of Lancaster, thenceforward became an
appanage of the royal family. The bailiff then became
the joint officer of lord and burgesses and the disputed
tolls and dues were leased to merchants at fixed rates.

By the end of the twelfth century, natural causes or
the go-ahead nature of its inhabitants had transformed
S. Botolph's 'untilled place where no man dwelt.' As
it happened it was singularly well situated to get the
most out of England's commercial prosperity, which in
the thirteenth and fourteenth centuries depended upon
her wool trade. Here was Botolph's Town, the port of
Lincoln (in itself a great commercial centre), in the
neighbourhood of wool-growing monasteries, such as
Swineshead, Spalding, Revesby, Croyland and Bardney;
with an easy passage across to the German and Flemish
coasts, where eager merchants awaited England's sup-
plies of wool. Nothing could have been better, and
Boston men soon took advantage of their happy situation. In 1205 (the year after Boston received its Charter
from King John) the Quindene, or tax of one fifteenth
levied on all merchandise, shows Boston paying £780,
second only to London which paid £856, and the
returns of money received as customs duty on wool,
wool-fells and skins, places Boston before London up
to 1290. The value of goods in Boston in 1205 was
£10,950, i.e., about £90,000 present value.

Boston, too, was in the forefront of progress, for it
was one of the first towns in England where wool was.

manufactured into cloth, an event in economic history showing the increased skill of the inhabitants. Most wool was exported as raw material in the twelfth century, but weavers are mentioned at Boston and a few other places, and it is in this connection that we get a glimpse of the kind of commercial trick common in those days. Hugh Bardolf and certain other of the King's justiciaries came to S. Botolph's in 1201 to seize certain cloths which were too narrow according to statute, 'but,' the record remarks, 'the merchants persuaded the justiciaries to leave them for a sum of money.'

Boston was defended by a wall and a moat on the north-east side of the river. The name Barditch indicates the position of the moat; Bargate on the east, Wormgate (a corruption of Witham-gate) on the north, and S. John's on the south, show the position of the old gates; while the west gate opened on a bridge across the river a little below the present bridge. Within the walls the housing question was being dealt with, for in 1272, 'William de Holgate took stone out of the King's quarry at Lincoln and sent it when squared by stone masons to build houses in Boston' (*Hundred Rolls*). Sometimes by gift, sometimes by purchase the monasteries rapidly acquired houses, where they could establish representatives to buy and sell in the busy little town. In 1247, Randulph de S. Botolph gave land in S. Botolph to the monks of Furness Abbey, but evidently it was awkwardly situated, for Randulph's son, Richard, granted the monks 'free ingress and egress through his garden.' Very considerable grants were made at various times to the nuns and brethren of the Gilbertine (mixed) Houses of Alvingham and Bullington (*Transcript of Charters*), and by the end of the century the Prior and Convent of Nocton, the Abbots of York, Louth Park, Fountains and

Leicester, and the Prior of Freiston (a cell of Croyland) all possessed houses in Boston. At the same time appear also merchants from Ypres, Cologne, Caen, Ostend, and Arras occupying houses, for at this period foreign trade was almost entirely in the hands of aliens.

Boston, in fact, was a centre both for home and foreign trade. In mediæval times home trade was carried on by means of markets and fairs—privileges granted to towns by charter. The market was a weekly and local event, the fair was an opportunity for laying in stores and wholesale buying and selling. Merchants and purchasers came from all parts, the fair was proclaimed and all other buying and selling in the neighbourhood ceased. Boston had several fairs, but the greatest was held about Midsummer and was said to have had its beginning· in the second year of King John (1200), while in 1218, it was extended to eight days after the Feast of S. John the Baptist (June 24th), and even then some merchants would have prolonged their stay and sales had they not been sternly sent on to Lynn. It was indeed a popular and cosmopolitan assembly, and the profits to the town in 1280 were £248—a very considerable sum in those days. Moreover the hiring out of booths and stalls erected for the exchange of merchandise, and of houses for the buyers and sellers to lodge in, as well as the collection of tolls and the fees of the local law courts, were all sources of wealth to those who could prove their right to them; and in this connection a characteristic dispute occurred in 1261, between Peter of Savoy, the unpopular uncle of Queen Eleanor, to whom Henry II had given the Honour of Richmond, and Robert de Tateshal, who held a manor and tenement in Boston. Robert, who was of a contentious nature and was constantly in

dispute on one account or another, complained that
Peter did not permit him to have in the times of the
Fairs of S. Botolph 'tronage and pesage of wool and
lead,' or the free exercise of his law court with fees
attaching to it, and 'that he could not freely hire out his
houses, stalls and plots during those times in the aforesaid vill to any merchants, at his will, without hindrance
from Peter and his bailiffs, as he ought to have them,
and is wont to have and hire them out, and as he and
his ancestors in the times of their King and in the times
of his predecessors, Kings of England, were wont to
have and hire them out' (*Final Concords*). The dispute
outwardly ended amicably, each agreeing to keep within
the bounds of his own fee, but in the next year Henry III
confirmed the grant of the manor and markets to Peter
of Savoy, and twenty years later the lord of the manor
was in dispute again about his tolls, this time with the
citizens of Lincoln, when 'the commons of Lincoln
would have withdrawn from the fair of Boston, but that
the sons of the mayor and two rich merchants arbitrated
and gave the lord of the manor a charter promising a
yearly rent of £10.' As to purchases at the fair—John,
minutely described as 'Son of Alan, son of Raingot of
Stickford' (about six miles north of Boston), stated that
'at the impulse of divine piety' he had granted to 'the
nuns of Ormsby to buy veils and cloaks at Boston,'
while Grosseteste, Bishop of Lincoln, in his 'Rules to
govern and guard the lands and hostel' of Margaret,
Countess of Lincoln (d. 1240), advises that 'at two
seasons of the year you make your purchases, your
wines and your wax at the Fair of S. Botolph'—but not
her 'robes,' which he considers would be better bought
at S. Ives. The Bolingbroke accounts show £124 spent
at S. Botolph's Fair, chiefly on cloth for the Earl of

THE OLD CELLS IN THE GUILDHALL, BOSTON

Lincoln, and the King's serjeant bought wine for the King's use, which on one occasion (1281) was all destroyed by a great fire so that Matthew de Columbarii (the keeper of the King's wine at Boston) had to settle his account with the Exchequer (*Close Rolls*).

When a toll in aid of repairing the walls was levied in 1285, the number and variety of the taxable articles in the town is entertainingly varied. We should already expect wool, grey cloth and russet cloth, wine and wax; perhaps also canvas and stockfish (since Boston was a seafaring place) and the more ordinary things of every-day life such as cheese, fat, butter, honey, sugar, salt, pepper, rabbits and tallow; to these add such accessories as rice and almonds and the spices, etc.—which figure so much in mediæval cookery—ginger, white cinnamon, cummin seed, liquorice, aniseed, picony roots or pinen-tum, cloves, nutmegs, mace, cubebs seed, safron, rosin and copperas, and the further miscellaneous collection of alum, lead, sulphur, potter's earth, bone of cuttle-fish, leather, whetstones, ashes, and pitch, incense, silk and fox skins. These last were taxed at the rate of one farthing the timber (i.e., forty skins), which shows that the present-day reynard is a gentleman of more consideration than his ancestors.

The importance and popularity of the town of S. Botolph and its Fair is evidenced by many a chance allusion. Thus, for example, Robert de Tateshal is to pay Maud de Scremby 6s. 8d. on the Feast of S. Botolph (June 17th), while the Nuns of Bullington received twenty acres of land of Philip Kyme and Hawise his wife on payment of 5s. at the Feast of S. Botolph; and occasionally such attractive entries occur as that of 'two clove gillyflowers' to be paid by William de Bedeford to Nicholas and Avicia de Tateshal on the

D

Feast of S. Botolph, or 'one rose' from John Bek to Robert de Wylghby at the Feast of the Nativity of S. John the Baptist, i.e., at the great Fair. But the Fair, which was so popular and brought so much trade, sometimes also gave the ne'er-do-wells their chance. Stephen, who came from the village of Coningsby, about twelve miles north-west of Boston, stole pennies from ships coming to Boston Fair (*Assize Rolls*, 1202). Sefrey Cote took unwarranted tolls from ships passing across the marsh, and having been dismissed under pledge he proceeded to tonsure his head and pass himself off as a clerk, as his friends, Richard Baccun, John, son of Jordan and Reginald Cote (perhaps his brother) could not deny. Richard de Kalmete was summoned to answer to the plea of Lucas de Batenturt for taking eleven tuns of wine and other goods to the value of £100 from the monastery of the Friars Minor. Richard of course denied that he had done anything of the kind, and as there is no record of the result of the enquiry we are left to end the story as we like.

Indeed, the thirteenth century, though a time of much robbery and murder, as the *Assize Rolls* bear witness, and the shifting and cosmopolitan character of a section of its inhabitants, as well as the suspicion with which the alien merchants were regarded, must often have caused many serious 'police' problems. More than once foreign merchants (especially Gascons) are accused of concealing felons and being paid for doing so, while there are many instances of murderers and others seeking sanctuary in the Church. Sometimes justice was swift and severe, as when William Wyeth de Gernon and Nicholas de Mundham were beheaded for 'slaying Peter de Martes in the field of S. Botolph,' but the reparation demanded for the death of two women, who very unpleasantly met their deaths by being scalded in tubs of verjuice, was no more than fines levied on certain vessels—the town perhaps was well rid of the women, and the crime was sufficiently corporate to make a light punishment possible. Yet Richard, son of Elye, met his death for stealing bread, and indeed the tolls of deaths for various offences between the years 1276 and 1300 is astonishing to the modern mind, which hesitates to inflict the death penalty even for the worst of crimes.

On one occasion the bedells found themselves in a curious dilemma. Under orders they had arrested a man who could not produce pledges of his identity and honesty and put him in the pillory. Here perhaps, being weary of this life, or perhaps under compulsion, he 'let his feet drop' and was hanged. The bedells might have thought this good riddance of bad rubbish, but unfortunately the matter was somehow brought to the notice of the King's justice, and the bedells were called upon to answer for what they had done. They pleaded that they had acted under instructions from Parisius and Jordan of S. Botolph (could this be the father of that John who had stood pledge for Sefrey Cote ?) and most luckily for them both these gentlemen were dead, so nothing could be proved, and we may hope that the bedells, though taken into custody, escaped lightly.

It was towards the end of the thirteenth century that Boston received several severe checks to its growing prosperity. Bad floods had occurred in the years 1236, 1254, and 1257, but in 1286 'an intolerable multitude of men, women and children were overwhelmed with the water, especially in the towne of Bostone, or Buttolp's towne, a great part whereof was destroyed,' and shortly before that, in 1281, a great fire (that enemy of mediæval times) had devastated the town (*Close Rolls*). But most serious of all disasters and outbreaks of violence was what is known as the Chamberlain Riot. 'A Justis (joust) was proclaimed in Boston, in the faire time in 1287, whereof one part came in the habyte of monks, the other in the sute of chanons, who had covenanted after the Justis, to spoile the faire; for the achieving of their purpose they fired the towne in three places; it was said the streams of gold, silver and metal, molten, ranne into the sea.' The merchants were robbed and many were murdered and the booty was carried off in ships which lay by the quay. 'The Caiptaine of this confederacye was Robert Chamberlain Esquire, who was hanged, but would never confess his fellows.'

In spite of disturbances and murders Boston, in ecclesiastical matters, was keeping well abreast of the times. Early in the thirteenth century, the Friars had made their appearance in England and Grosseteste, Bishop of Lincoln, who was in the forefront of ecclesiastical advance and church reform, wrote immediately on his consecration to the Provincial of the Friars Preachers (Dominicans) asking for assistance, and also to the Friars Minor (Franciscans), urging the needs of his diocese, 'the widest and most densely populated in England.'

The Dominicans were settled at Oxford (then in the Lincoln diocese) in 1221, and at Boston, Lincoln and Stamford in 1222, and Grosseteste personally proceeded, with their help, to carry out his reforms. He writes : 'When the clergy and the people were assembled I myself was accustomed to preach the Word of God to the Clergy, and some Friar, either Preacher or Minorite, to the people; at the same time four friars were employed in hearing confessions and enjoining penances; and when the children had been confirmed on that and the following day, I and my clerks gave our attention to inquiries, corrections and reformations, such as belong to the office of inquiry. In my first circuit of this sort,' he adds, 'some came to me to find fault with these proceedings, saying, "My Lord, you are doing a new and unaccustomed thing"—To whom I answered "Every new thing which instructs and advances a man is a blessed new thing." '

Grosseteste's vigorous methods may have been deprecated at first, but at any rate in Boston there were probably many who agreed with his radical sentiments, and the Friars obtained much popularity and patronage. The Dominicans were easily first in the field, but in 1293, the Carmelites (White Friars) were licensed by Bishop Sutton to have a chantry in the oratory of S. Botolph, and Master Geoffrey de Vezano, a papal nuncio, who was Rector of the parish church in 1299, gave the Friars permission to have a church, house and churchyard in his parish, to celebrate divine service and bury brethren in the churchyard.

The house of the Carmelites was in what is now Fydell Crescent. It is certain that the Franciscans (Grey Friars) had a house in Boston in 1268, for it was in that year that Luke de Batenturt complained of Richard de Kalmete's robbery of wine from the Grey Friars' church, but the founder and date of foundation are unknown. The site of this Friary was near the Grammar School. Finally, the Austin Friars were established before 1307, since in that year Nicholas atte Gate had licence to give lands in Boston to them.

There was a tradition that the Friary in what is now (Skirbeck Road) was established by the well-known

Boston family of Tilney, but whether this was so or not cannot be determined.

The Knights of the Order of S. John of Jerusalem found, too, their place in the life of the town. Sir Thomas de Multon (lord of the manor of Skirbeck and bailiff of the Honour of Richmond) had, in 1200, given the Knights certain rights and founded a hospital for twelve poor folk in Skirbeck, and the house of the Knights was just outside S. John's Gate, on ground which is still known as S. John's Churchyard.

There were doubtless many in bustling Boston ready to endorse Grosseteste's declaration, that 'every new thing which instructs and advances a man is a blessed new thing,' and so, as the thirteenth century passes into the fourteenth, we find the old monastery of S. Botolph left in a back water, and the newer religious orders establishing themselves more and more in the affections of the town and its neighbourhood.

Bequests 'to the four Orders of Friars in Boston' are frequent in Lincolnshire wills for the next hundred years and more, generally with the added injunction 'to pray for me,' or more explicitly as Sir Thomas Cumberworth puts it, 'to say . . . three messys of ye holy gost.'

The churches of the Friars and of the Knights of S. John became the ordinary burial place for certain of their patrons. The tombs of the Knight and lady now in S. Botolph's are the only ones which survive from the Church of S. John. In the Church of the Grey Friars lay 'the Montevelles Gentlemen and six or seven of the Withams Gentlemen also.' Leland (the sixteenth-century antiquary) tells us, that the Grey Friars, who were always connected with the commercial classes, came under the patronage of the foreign merchants, for 'the merchants of the Steelyard were wont greatly to haunt Boston and the Grey Friars took them in a manner for founders of their house and many Esterlings were buried there,' and still one memorial of them remains with us in the black marble slab and incised figure of Wisselus Smalenburg, a merchant of Munster, which is now in the Church of S. Botolph, but formerly was (doubtless with others) in the church of the Grey Friars. Wisselus is represented in a full-length figure standing under a canopy with his hands joined in prayer and his feet resting on a dog. The inscription tells the exact day of his death and asks prayers for his soul.

The Black Friars were perhaps more aristocratic in their patrons, for 'in the Black Freres lay one of the noble Huntingfields and was late taken up hole, and a leaden Bull of Innocentius, Bishop of Rome' (Innocent VI, 1362–70) 'about his neck,' doubtless that very 'Sir William, Lord of Huntyngfeld,' at whose burial there was an unseemly disturbance, for the Bishop wished to be present, but about two hundred friars barred the chancel and defended it against the Bishop and his retinue with swords and arrows. The Bishop withdrew, but made an attempt next day to come and offer mass for the soul of the Lord of Huntingfield. The friars, however, armed themselves with heavy stones, ascended to the belfry (i.e., the tower over the entrance to the choir), established themselves round the gallery and prepared to hurl down their missiles on the heads of any who attempted to enter. Public proclamation of this insult to the Bishop was made and letters of protest were at once despatched to the Archbishop of Canterbury and to the Provincial of the Friars Preachers (*Linc. Epis. Reg*), but exactly how the Friars were called to order is not recorded.

Indeed the Dominicans just at this time in Boston appear to have been turbulent neighbours. It was only three years later that a section of rebellious friars led certain other people to scale the walls of the Friary with ladders, break in doors and windows and assault Prior Roger Dymoke—a man of well-known family—and his friars in their beds. Prior Dymoke promptly ordered the bells to be rung, and the townsfolk, awakened by the call of fire, came promptly to his aid. At this time Strensale was Rector of S. Botolph's and we may wonder, as we look at his brass in the church, whether he took any part in vanquishing the rebels. His predecessor, John Baret, had so assaulted Friar Simon of the Order of Black Friars that his life had hung in the balance (Pat. Ed. III).

The fourteenth century in Boston saw the building of the main structure of the present great church of S. Botolph's: the foundation of fifteen or more Gilds, and the increase in number and influence of foreign merchants. It is in this century, perhaps, that Boston reaches the height of its prosperity, but before the century passes into the next there are signs that this prosperity is already on the wane. Up till 1369 Boston was the port of Lincoln, but in 1369 it was made a staple town, which meant that now wool could be brought direct from all parts instead of having to pass first through Lincoln. The Merchants of the Staple, though hampered by restrictions, had a monopoly of trade, which lasted to the end of the century. Every merchant who was not a staple merchant was necessarily an Adventurer, but it was not until 1406 that the Merchant Adventurers were granted a charter by Henry IV.

While wool was shipped abroad, large shipments of wine continued to come into England via Boston. In

1333 the King's butler had permission to collect customs of 2s. a tun of wine. Robberies of wine are recorded in 1320 and 1322. The former of these was carried out by Flemings, the latter by men of Sandwich, Winchelsea, and Greenwich, for in those days the rivalry between one port and another was as great as that between English merchants and aliens. The men of Sandwich were almost as much foreigners to the Bostonians as the men of Ypres.

Great quantities of wine were shipped to Boston from Bordeaux. King John of France, for instance, receiving 140 tuns while he was a prisoner in England in Edward III's reign.

The Fair, though still popular, appears to have been rather less profitable to the town, for in 1331 the profits are estimated at £100 only. The Fair accounts show the following entries: Front houses, £7 10s. 10d.; twenty stalls, £11 14s. 2d.; 'Royal booths,' £28 13s. 4d.; Houses of Merchants of Ypres, £20; of Cologne, £25 10s.; of Caen, £24 6s. 8d., etc.

In 1331 the 'Lords of the Fair' were in trouble for attempting to prolong the Fair beyond its legal limits. A commission of inquiry was held as to 'whether the Lords of the Fair of S. Botolph held the fair beyond the time fixed by charter . . . also whether merchants, as well native as foreign, tarried to the said fair and sold their goods beyond the limited time, in manifest contempt of the King, and contrary to the Law' (5 Edward III).

In other ways, too, the men of S. Botolph's appear to have been too independent in spirit, for though 'the Mayor et les bons gens' caused a levy for the King's service abroad to muster at Peterborough in 1324 and other subsequent years and paid large subsidies, yet in

1348 'the King issued a patent grant of pardon to a great many men of the town of S. Botolph for their felonies and conspiracies, and having assumed the regal power in the said town' (*Patent Rolls*). The cause of this may have been dissatisfaction at the prolonged wars (*Victoria County History*), but more probably the levy by Boston bailiffs of duties on Lincoln merchandise about which the townspeople of Lincoln petitioned the King. But these differences were short lived, and in 1359 Boston furnished men, and as many as seventeen ships to the navy—a greater number than Portsmouth, Hull, Harwich or Lynn.

Improvements in the town continued, as for example the paving of the town in 1313 and 1320 (*Grants of Tolls*, 6 Ed. II).

In 1309 the foundation of the great church was laid on the Monday after S. John the Baptist's Day, when the town was full to overflowing for the great fair. Perhaps this event marks the height of Boston's greatness, for the romantic tradition that the foundations were laid on wool sacks show in the simplest way that the church was the outcome of Boston's prosperity, and it is a testimony to the same fact that the foundation stone was laid by Dame Margaret Tilney, wife of one of the great Boston merchants, who was assisted by Richard Stephenson, a merchant. John Treesdale was Rector, and at that time the life of the town centred round the great church and found its religious and social expression in the famous Gilds of the town.

It is worth while to go into some detail in the effort to conjure up a picture of the richness, the colour and the activity of this gild life centreing day by day in S. Botolph's, with its yearly round of festival and fast, its almost daily commemoration of departed benefactors, its 'pageants' (Gild plays) and processions—the meeting place, in fact, of all citizens.

There seem certainly to have been five incorporated gilds and eight lesser ones, though they may not all have existed at the same time.[1] How far they were connected with the regulation of industry cannot be exactly determined, but it may be supposed that they filled much the same position as the gilds of other towns, and in like manner lost their control of industry in the course of the fifteenth century and became benefit and fashionably pious societies.

Many of the records of the Boston Gilds have been lost, and the Inventory of S. Mary's Gild alone remains to give some idea of the appearance of one only of the 'Houses' or halls where the gilds met for business and social purposes, while the Register of Corpus Christi furnishes an idea of the popularity of these gilds.

There seems little doubt that the Gild of Blessed Mary was the Merchant Gild of the town, i.e., the gild to which all merchants belonged and which had its industrial, as well as its religious and social duties. It was founded as early as 1260 by Andrew de Gote, Walter Tumby, Galfrid de la Goters, Robert Leland and Hugh Spaynge of S. Botolph's (*Kings Writ of Inquiry*, 1389). The MS. of the Writ of Inquiry is much decayed and in parts undecipherable, but it is possible to make out that there were certain charitable and pious purposes in the foundation, as for instance that a thousand loaves and a thousand herrings were to be given away annually

---

[1] *Incorporated Gilds.*—Gild of Blessed Virgin Mary; Corpus Christi or S. Botolph's; SS. Peter and Paul; S. George; Trinity.

Lesser Gilds.—S. Catherine; 'Postill' or Apostles; Holyrood; Gild of the Fellowship of Heaven; Gild of the Seven Martyrs; Ascension; SS. Simon and Jude; S. James and possibly S. Anne.

at the Feast of the Purification (February 2nd), that candles should be burned before the altar of the Blessed Virgin, torches carried at funerals and that a priest should say Mass daily at about 9 a.m. in S. Botolph's, taking about an hour to do so.

The MS. certifies that the Gild had no lands or goods except the ornaments of the church, but throughout the next hundred and fifty years gifts and privileges were showered upon it.

Pope Sixtus IV, Nicholas V, and Pius II granted privileges and pardons, but apparently Pope Julius II had to be approached with great circumspection, for according to Fox (Acts and Monuments), Geoffrey Chambers was sent to Antwerp to enlist the good offices of Thomas Cromwell, and he in his turn went to Rome, and, having entertained the Pope with 'gelly junkets,' preferred his request. The Pope was rendered amenable and granted certain privileges, among which was the important concession that all who went to the Chapel of Our Lady in S. Botolph's at Whitsun, Corpus Christi, the Feasts of the Nativity and of the Assumption of Our Lady, the Feast of S. Michael, or on the First Sunday in Lent, 'should have pardon no lesse than if they themselves had visited the stations of Rome,' or if they could not come to S. Botolph's, but went to their own parish church and there said one Pater and one Ave Maria, they should have the same remission. Or again, whoever came every Friday to the Chapel of Our Lady, should have as much remission as if he went to the Chapel of Our Lady of Scala Caeli. Here, therefore, was set up the shrine known as the Scala Caeli, to approach which penitents had to ascend the steps on their knees. There were only three such shrines in England, the other two being in King Henry VII's

Chapel, Westminster, and the Chapel of Our Lady of the Augustine Friars at Norwich.

When the Scala Caeli was set up in the Lady Chapel of S. Botolph's, the Chapel presented a very different appearance from that which it presents to-day. It was separated from the nave by a wooden screen and another screen with a rood and loft crossed the aisle from the second nave pillar to the south wall. These screens no doubt were fine specimens of fourteenth-century workmanship, and together with the rest of the Chapel were probably richly coloured.

Some quotations from the Inventory of the Gild will show the richness of the furnishings and vestments. In the worn and stained MS. we may read as follows:[1] 'ffirst an altar cloth of white damaske with Egles standynge uppon bookes with scripture on there hedes with a frontell of the same therto belongynge. Item an altar cloth of blew damask with this letter M crowned with a frontell of the same belongynge thereunto. Item an altar cloth of red silke powthered with flowres called boston with a frontell of red powthered with pehennes.'

Another frontell, the gift of Mr. John Robynson, was 'of tawney damask with Egles standynge on bookes with the arms of the said Mr. Robynson in the myddes of the altar cloth with a frontell of the same thereto belonginge havynge the seide armes at eu'y end of the seide frontell.'

Curtains and hangings enclosed the altar at the back and sides and adorned the walls. As for example, 'a peire of curteynes of white sarcynett steyned (painted) with two ymages, one of our lady and the other of

---

[1] In quotations from the Inventory the old spelling has been retained, but not the abbreviations.

gabriell with birdes standynge on books: seven tables with scriptures upon them to hange on the altares . . . and sixteen banners to hange abaute the altares in the time of the Jubilee,[1] whereof fourteen of them be with the popes armes and two with the Kinges : a steyned banner cloth of Lynyn cloth with the ymage of our lady and certeyn ymages of men and women knelyng before her: a steynad streamar of lynyn cloth' and 'dyverce other paynted clothes with stories and betail'es hangyng aboute the queyr of our lady.'

The statue of the Blessed Virgin, which stood in the Chapel, possessed a variety of mantles, one for example, of 'cloth of tysseu purfild aboute with powther armyn of the gift of Maistres thorneborow.'

The vestments were of equal magnificence. Thus, 'a whole vestment for a preist with deacon and sub-deacon of white damaske with Egles of golde standinge on bookes berynge scriptures on their hedes and orfrays of a story of our ladie with all other things to the seide vestyment belongynge: Item a whole vestment for preist, deacon and subdeacon of white damaske pow-deryd with flowres of silke & gold with orfraies of red velvett powderyd with silk and gold with all other thinges to the seide vestyment belongynge.'

John Cowell and Johan, his wife, gave 'a whole vestyment of blak velvett for preist deacon and sub-deacon with orfraies of tent work with the scriptures' and their names written on them. Mr. John Robynson completed his former gift by adding 'a vestment of tawny damaske with Egyles standinge on bookes with this lettre M crowned with a orfray of red velvett . . . havinge his armes uppon it.' Thomas Awbre contributed

[1] A period during which the Pope granted plenary indulgences to all persons, who, having confessed and received Holy Communion, visited certain churches. Usually celebrated every fiftieth year.

a 'vestyment of blew with golden birds and angels wrought on the same with a orfray of ymages wrought with coper and gold.'

Mr. Thomas Robertson, when he was alderman, saw to it that the vestment chest was enriched by the addition of a vestment of 'greene velvett and white damask with a orfray of greene velvett with a rose of gold in the myddes of the crosse' and another of 'white satten of brigges (Bruges) powthered with flowers with a orfray of blak velvett and greene satten of brigges.'

The altars and shrines were furnished with candlesticks of silver gilt or copper gilt ('latton'). In the Lady Chapel, possibly above the altar, stood 'a crosse of sylver and gylt with two branches and two ymages therupon standynge; that is to saye, the ymage of our Blessed Ladye and the ymage of Saynt John gylt and enameled weynge in the whole on hundred and eighty four onzes with a sufferayne (sovereign) of gold thereto nayled and offered by John Rede.'

The 'shafte of sylver for the same crosse with roll of gylt' was two and a half yards high and ornamented with 'three knotts gylt of the wyche knotts everyone hath six roses enamelid with asure.'

'A great Egle of latton standynge on thre lions of latton' stood 'in the myddes of the queyr' for the precentors. 'Another great lecterone' from which probably the Gospel was sung out of that 'gospell book' which had a 'cace . . . of sylur and gilte with certeyn ymages thereon gravyn of the gift of Mʳ John Bevell of London,' the Mass being sung sometimes from 'the pryncypall masse-booke, with two claspes of sylver and gylt with two roses with pynnys of sylver gylt,' sometimes from 'another grete Masse-booke with claspes of sylver gylt.'

The Alderman, when he attended Mass officially, knelt on 'a carpet with two cushions of fustian in naples' and wore a chaplet (cloak) of red velvet 'with one great owche[1] in the front of the same of pure gold and in the same be sett three gret perles with six turkaces (turquoises). Item uppon the same chaplett eight great owches of pure gold with eight balesez (rubies) set in the myddes of each of them and garneshid with two chesses of perle abowte every of them five stones. Item sixteen other owches but litill ones of perle and stone. Item likewise in the hyndermore parte of the seide chaplett one gret owche of sylver and gylte garnyshid with perle in the circute.'

The 'chamberlaynes' attending wore chaplets of 'blew velvett powderyd with sterres of gold with letters M and lilies of perle' and carried 'verges' (wands) paynted and harnesid at both ends with silur.' Surely on these great festival days the 'childer,' dressed in their 'small albes,' who served the priests at the altar, carried the 'shippe' containing the incense or rang the 'bell of sylver' *'ad deferendum coram corpore Christi'* and the 'torchberars' in their 'sirplesis of lynyn cloth,' who carried candles on 'torchheads of wood gilte, with gilded shaftes for the same,' in such surroundings could never have felt bored, even when devotion failed at the length of the service or the heat of the day.

Leland remarks specially upon the music of S. Botolph's, which he says was 'served so with singing, and that of cunning men, as no parish in all England. The society and brotherhood longing to this church causeth this.'

The Gild accounts[2] (1514–46) bear this out. From

---

[1] Owche. An ornament composed of a jewel of precious stones set in gold and silver.

[2] Mostly lost about 1875.

THE GRAMMAR SCHOOL, BOSTON

them we learn that there was a choir school and that
Mr. Westewoode (Master of the Choristers) was provided with a house and garden and was paid £13 6s. 8d.,
besides £3 6s. 8d. for teaching singing. The organist,
John Wendon, received £13 6s. 8d., the singing clerks
were paid as much as the chaplains, while the choristers
were given 'le brodecloth' (for their gowns) 'tunics,
birretts' (caps), 'shirts, shoes,' stockings and all other
clothing, besides 'le comys' (combs) at 2d. each, a pair
of knives and 'le baggs' to keep them in.

John Broke, who was 'keeper of the Lady Choir,'
who scoured candlesticks, strewed the floor of the
chapel with rushes and slept in the vestry in winter,
was paid 1s. 4d. extra 'for seeing choristers say their
mattins every day.'

We may gather something of the daily activity in
S. Botolph's from the will of Mr. John Robynson,
whose gifts enriched the Gild. He directs that 'two
honest and discreet priests of good conversation, who
can sufficiently sing their plainsong, shall say mass daily,
at the altar of Our Lady in the church in Boston. One
of the said priests to say mass at the aforesaid at six
of the clock in the morning daily, so that it be done
before seven, and the other priest to say mass at the
same place between eight and nine in the morning
daily, so that it be done before nine and the usual masses
of the day be not letted by the said masses . . . and the
said priests when they are at mass at their going to the
first lavatory' (washing of hands) 'shall turn them to the
people and with a loud voice pray for the soul of John
Robynson with the prayer de profundis and a collect
and one of the said priests when they have said mass
after S. John's Gospel in their albes shall go to the
graves of the father and mother of the said John Robynson

E

and also his grave and say the de profundis and also the collect . . . and cast holy water upon the said graves.'

Obits (Masses for the souls of the departed said on the anniversaries of their deaths) were a great feature in the gild regulations. The Register of the Corpus Christi Gild directs that 'there shall follow in the said register a kalendar, with a space opposite each month to register the names of the brothers and sisters of the said gild who shall die and especially of those benefactors to the gild who have given or shall bequeath any memorial to the Gild, or of whose obit the alderman and brethren hold annual commemoration. And lastly, in the said register, shall be recorded the rule of all obits by the alderman and brethren to be held and celebrated.' Often these were proclaimed by a bellman, who, accompanied by the sacristan of the Gild, made a circuit of the town and called upon the citizens for their prayers, as, for example, in the following manner : 'Ye shall pray for the souls of William Reede of Boston and Alice, Margaret and Anne that were his wives and brother and sisters in Corpus Christi Gild, brother and sisters in S. Mary's Gild, brother and sisters in S. Peter's Gild, brother and sisters in the Trinity Gild, brother and sisters in S. George's Gild, brother and sisters in S. Katharine's Gild tomorne shall be their yere day.' In the case of John and Eleanor Robinson the obits were to be held on the Feast of S. Dennis in the Chapel of Corpus Christi in S. Botolph's and 'annually in the Chapel of our Blessed Lady in Boston on the first day of March or thereabouts during a term of ninety years solemnly by note' (sung) 'both of quire and mass of requiem, at the which mass the alderman of the fraternity if present at the said mass of requiem shall take eight pennies or

the alderman officiating in his stead shall take them and
every person present at the said mass who has been an
alderman shall receive 4d. And at the said obit there
shall be expended yearly 40s. to be given to the alderman, priests, and other persons attending such mass.'
At such obits would be used to cover the catafalque one
of the herse-cloths listed in the Inventory, perhaps the
'principall herse cloth of red tysseu with valance of
blew velvett brotheryd with venys gold and ymages of
the resurrexion frynged with silke and lyned with blew
bukram,' or the one with 'ymages of the assumption of
our lady with lile pottes with valance of blak woorsted.'
John Robynson had given an altar cloth 'of blak damask
. . . with his armes standyng in the myddes thereof
with a frontell of the same . . . having the seide armes
at every end.' And the priests might be vested in the
'whole vestyments for priest deacon and subdeacon of
blak woorsted with orfraies of red woorsted with
garters and scriptures.'

The Gild was of course rich in altar vessels. It
possessed, for example, three silver gilt chalices and
patens, one being for use on 'fferiall daies,' the 'beste'
described as 'the gyfte of Thomas Awbrie' and another
as having 'a gilte knopp havynge six roses,' and three
smaller chalices. Two silver basens, one 'with a rose
in the myddes gilt with gryffyn hedes of the gift of
Thomas Awbrie' and the other 'with a rose in the
myddis gilte with the ymage of our lady theryn gravyn
and enamelid with aswre.' Five censars and 'shippes,'
one the gift of Thomas Awbrie: 'cruettes of silver and
parcell gilte,' of which, however, one (the gift of Thomas
Awbrie) unfortunately 'lackes his lidd,' and four paxes,
one the gift of Thomas Awbrie and another of John
Reede.

The books belonging to the Gild included mass books, manuals, breviaries (one of which 'Sir Otnell toke away'), 'dirige bookes' and grailes (containing passages for singing at High Mass), some of which lay 'chayned . . . in the stawles in our Lady's Quire.' Besides these there were 'a booke of lawe called Codex; an Englyshe booke called Liber de divinis virtutibus the gifte of Dame Joan Gryymescrofte sometyne nonne of Staynfeyld: a booke called Scholasticus historica':[1] and 'a booke called Constitutionis Provinciall.'[2]

The Hall of S. Mary's Gild is what is now known as the Guildhall, and there also the Gild possessed many valuables as well as household effects. It is not always possible to make out from the Inventory how much was kept at the Church and how much at the Hall, but it seems clear that there was a Chapel at the Hall and in it 'a table of alabaster,' a statue of Our Lady in alabaster, a tabernacle and pyx, altar cloths and vestments, bell and candlesticks. The Hall was hung with 'steyned hangyngs' and lighted by five 'candlestykes hangynge like potts whereof the hyghest hath five branches and the others three.' On a table lay a parchment 'noted with antem of our Lady and three collecs,' perhaps for use at the time of the Gild banquets, when we may think of the brethren seated at the 'eight tables on the north side' and the 'seven tables on the south side' covered with 'tabill lynen marked with this letter M crowned.'

The light from the five 'candlestykes hangynge like potts' shone on the 'laver of latton hangynge with a

---

[1] Scholasticus historica super Novum Testamentum of Peter Comestor, one of the most popular books of the Middle Ages.

[1] Provinciall seu Constitutiones Angliæ, by William Lyndwode, sometime Bishop of S. David's, and buried in the crypt of S. Stephen's Chapel, Westminster.

chayne of yron' and on tables loaded with the gild plate, which would rival the college plate of to-day. Here are some of the pieces: Two moses (probably dishes), one is 'a great mose with a fete with the ymage of the Ascension of our Lord of silver and gilte of the gift of Harmond Staynford,' another of silver gilt 'enameled with an ymage of our Lady and another ymage knelynge before her.' Among the nine mazars (maple-wood bowls) there is one 'with a sengle band with a prynt in the botham gilt with an ymage of Allmyghti God sittyn at the judgement in the myddes of the four evangelists of the gift of James barbor,' another 'with a prynt in the bothom of the passion of saynt Thomas the martir,' a third 'with a prynt of the vernacle[1] in the bothom of the gift of John Welles of Lyn,' a fourth 'with a prynt in the bothom of silver and gilte of the salutacion of our Lady with a lili pott,' others less ornate and some with 'no prynte in the bothom.' Of the standing cups one was held 'in pawne for the white friars' as also was a 'flat boll with a cover of silver,' which argues that the friars were not too prosperous at that time. The other standing cup was a fine piece 'standinge uppon thre angelles with a great knopp above enamelid with asure,' weighing 46½ ounces. Two goblets, two salts and a gilt spoon were the gift of John Robynson. There were two dozen 'silver spoons havinge this letter M in the end of the stele of them,' twelve of which were 'delyuyd to the chaplaynes of the gilde,' as also was 'a pece of silver with a prynt of the ymage of oure lady in the bothom of the gift of William aston of caster.' The 'huntynge horne harnesid with silver with a bukkill and XVIII barres and a synkfoile

---

[1] S. Veronica's handkerchief on which was a representation of the face of our Lord.

with a littil chayne and a pendent of silver of the gift of davy wragby sometyme bayly of wragby and one of the brethren of the gilde' was 'valuyd by estymacion' as also probably were two boxes of ivory, one 'bound with . . . silur and withyn the same XXXIII small perles' and the other 'with an ymage of our lady of yvery theryn closid . . . enclosid in a purse of neilde werke.' Other miscellaneous possessions included 'an A and S of golde joyned to gether with a stone in it delyuyd to this gilde bi Mr Malyvery in payment of his brother hood,' ten 'bedes of lambr' (amber) and two cassildens (chalcedony) with 'a strynge of silk and I tas shell and III silur gymes and I rynge of silur gilte hangynge by the same.'

In the two kitchens of the Hall were great brass and iron pots weighing as much as 100 lbs., 95 lbs., 60 and 50 lbs., pewter and laten to the weight of 500 lbs., three 'great broches' (spits) 'of yron,' each $3\frac{1}{2}$ yards long suspended from 'a payre of cobbards of yron' weighing 23 lbs., and a beam of yron with four leaden weights of 56, 28, 28 and 14 lbs. In the lower kitchen was a great vessel of lead, 'a hen cage with a shelfe withyn,' ale tubs and pots, baskets and elaborate paraphernalia for making bread. In the buttery 'a pryck to hang clothes on, a bynke to sett ale potts on,' cupboards (one for the broken meat to be given away in alms), chests, trenchers, pewter plates, dishes, 'sawcers,' a 'quantitye of tabill linen' and so on.

The 'parlair' seems to have been hung with 'a hanging steyned with birds and beasts' and simply furnished with 'a short playne table,' chairs, a 'buffett stoole,' fire irons and three 'racons' (a word still used in Lincolnshire which means a cross-bar and pot-hooks).

The bedrooms were still simpler, containing only

'a peyre of bed stocks, presses of waynscott, a bynke to ley colis' (clothes) 'in' and 'formes.'

The Gild had its important relics, which were as follows: 'Fyrst there is a relike of part of the fynger of Saint Ann, closed in a hande of sylver and gylt, the wiche hande of sylver with the foresayde parte of the fynger is set in a sertin pece of sylver and gylte; to the lawde and prayse of Almightie God, whiche hande with parte of the fynger aforesayde and sylver and gold therunto anexed was the gifte of Thomas Awbre, and weys in the whole six ounces.

'Another relike, honowred with sylver and gylt with a certe bone of Saynt Crystine with certen other relikes of the same bone inclused; of the gyft of Robert Coke prest and weyinge five and a half ounces.

'A relike inclused in sylver and parcell gylt that is to saye a poynt of the fynger of Saynt Ann with serten bones of the Innocents; weyinge in the whole five ounces and a half.

'A cace of sylver and parcel gylt in the whyche is conteyned part of the stone of Mownte Calvery and partt of the stone from whyche Cryste ascended into Heven, and a parte of the stone of the sepulchre of Cryste weyinge in the wholl four ounces and a half.

'Another cace of sylver and gylte; in the whyche is conteyned parte of the mylke of our Lady weyinge in the wholl four ounces and a half.'

Space will not permit to write further of the Gild beloved of Thomas Awbrie, John Rede, John Robynson and many other brethren and benefactors, but before leaving the subject of the Gilds which played such a prominent part in the daily life of the Boston citizens we must turn for a moment to the Register of the Corpus Christi Gild.

The position of the Hall of this Gild is only recorded by the name Corpus Christi Lane, which turns off Wide Bargate, and the position of the Chapel in S. Botolph's is unknown, but we know that there were six chaplains of the Gild at a stipend of £5 6s. 8d. each. All the Rectors of Boston, from John Barett (1316) to John Mabledon (1524) were members of this Gild, and to begin with the membership was wide and distinguished, but in the fifteenth and sixteenth centuries, when the Gilds became more ecclesiastical the membership decreased. The Gild was founded May 8th, 1335, by Gilbert Alilunde, a merchant of S. Botolph's, who was in office as Alderman until 1349 and died May, 1353.

On the first register there are thirty names, twenty-six of whom were Boston men, the names including such familiar ones as Sutton, Latoner, Brass, Smith, Horn, Kattison, Travenor, Butt, Bussey, Henry and Drope. Very soon the Gild became popular, and by 1343, the numbers had risen to 104 and the names include that of Blanche, Duchess of Lancaster, Alicia Lacy, Countess of Lincoln, John de Skirbeck, who (though evidently of Boston country) was butler to Edward, Prince of Wales (the Black Prince), and several of the well-known Boston family of Spayne.

A new charter was granted to the Gild in 1349, and the members under the new ordinance include King Edward III, 'brother and establisher of the Gild,' Queen Philippa, 'his most benign consort,' and Edward, 'the victorious Prince of Wales.'

The Gild membership could hardly rise higher than this, but a few more interesting names may be noticed: William Harcourt (1366);[1] Lord d'Eresby; Lady Margaret Howard (1380); Lord and Lady Beaumond (1390);

---

[1] The dates given are not always the year of entry into the Gild.

Thomas, Duke of Exeter, 'princeps graciosus'; Thomas, Lord de la Warre, Canon of Lincoln; Henry, Bishop of Winchester (1420); Richard, Lord Welles and Willoughby (1470); Jacqueline, Duchess of Bedford, sister-in-law to Henry V; John Bossele, Bishop of Lincoln and Chancellor of England; Thomas Dairs, Grand Master of the Knights of S. John of Jerusalem in England; Peter, Bishop of London; John Viscount Welles and Cecilia his wife, the daughter of Edward IV; William, Bishop of Carlisle; Margaret, Countess of Richmond and Derby, mother of Henry VII. Famous Boston names occur constantly. Spaynes, Rochefords, Henrys, Withams, Pinchbecks, Sibseys, Kymes, Redes and Robynsons figure as aldermen, and there are such a confusing number of Tilneys that it would seem as if every member of every branch of the family must have belonged.

In earlier days, at least, the Gild was not exclusive, for besides many merchants of Boston and elsewhere, whom we should expect to find as members, there are also such entries as 'Agnes servant of Simon Do wode'; 'Helwyse, servant to John Rochford'; 'The Master of the School in Boston'; 'Matilda Manfleete, Mistress of the School in Boston.' A few foreign names occur and among them that of Gerard Delarmonde, Easterling, but they are by no means in proportion to the increase in number and influence of foreign merchants, which is a striking feature in the fourteenth and fifteenth centuries.

We have only to glance at the Stump to convince ourselves that this influence was real. Whoever the master-builder of that great steeple may have been, it is evident that he had in mind the great belfreys across the sea. In 1336 a patent grant of protection was issued for fourteen ships and a number of German merchants coming to the Fair. Possibly among their number was

Wisselus Smalenburg, who died only four years later. He and others may have been merchants of the Hanseatic League, for Münster was a Hanse town, and it was in this century that the League secured a Steelyard (fortified warehouse) and dock in Boston.[1] The League reached the height of its power in the fifteenth century. Its monopoly of trade became more and more galling to English merchants, and when it became a factor in the political disputes of the Wars of the Roses and used this opportunity to extort enormous privileges, the hatred of English merchants increased fourfold. In Boston this smouldering hatred burst forth in 1470, when there was a riot in which a merchant named Humphrey Littlebury killed one of the Easterlings.

This was the same year as the Rebellion of Lancastrians in Lincolnshire, and though Boston had, as far as we know, no part in this, any more than most towns had part in the events of the Wars of the Roses, yet it may be noted that the object of this 'rebellion' was to put George, Duke of Clarence, on the throne, that the Easterlings supported Edward IV and that he had restored the Steelyard in Boston to them, that George, Duke of Clarence, owned a manor in Boston, and that Richard Lord of Welles, who was one of the Lancastrian leaders in the rebellion, was that very year admitted a member of the Corpus Christi Gild. Who knows what discussions and disputes may not have arisen between English and foreign merchants in Boston over the rival claims of York and Lancaster? High words may have led to riot and riot brought about murder. At any rate, Leland attributes the decline of Boston's prosperity to this unfortunate murder. He says 'One Humphrey

---

[1] The large swimming bath at the Public Baths is all that remains of this dock.

Littlebyri, merchant of Boston, did kill one of the
Easterlings, whereupon rose much controversy, so that
at last the Easterlings left their course of merchants to
Boston.'

Natural causes, however, also contributed to destroy
the prosperity of Boston. The little harbour was
silting up, just when ships were getting bigger. Again,
Boston had always been subject to floods, and one of
the worst on record occurred in 1467, only three years
before the Littlebury riot. Ingulphus, the Chronicler
of Croyland, says, 'there was scarcely a house or building
but what the streams of water made their way and
flooded through it. Nor must it be supposed that this
happened hurriedly and in a cursory manner only; but
continually during a whole month, the waters either
stood there without flowing off, or else being agitated
by strong gusts of wind, swelled and increased still
more and more day after day. Nor on this occasion
did the embankments offer an effectual resistance, but
on the contrary, though materials had been brought
from other quarters for the purpose of strengthening
them, they proved of very little service for that purpose;
however diligently the work must have been attended
to in the daytime, as the waters swelled and rose, the spot
under repair was completely laid bare during the night.'

Under Henry VII it seemed possible that the decline
of Boston's prosperity might be arrested. The King's
policy was to free England from her bondage to the
Hanseatic League. Early in the reign a council was
held at which the question of the flood danger and the
silting up of the river at Boston was discussed.

In 1500, a Flemish engineer, a certain Mahave Hall,
was fetched over to construct a dam and sluice, which
for the time being proved successful, but only for the

time being. Besides, with the discovery of the New World the trade centre gradually shifted from east to west, and Boston, with its little silted-up harbour on the wrong coast, could not hope to hold its own in the modern trade of the sixteenth century. It was only very slowly that this became evident, and the council in Henry VII's reign was only the first of the Tudor efforts to set Boston on its legs again and restore it to its mediæval glory.

But the sixteenth century is, on the whole, a pathetic period in the town's history. The Reformation came and with it the stripping away of the outward signs of the artistic and religious richness of mediæval life. By this time the four Friaries were reduced to great straits. Leland was unable to visit them in 1539 on account of a pestilence, but he records that the Black, White and Austin Friars 'piteously lamented their poverty, and knowing not how to live till their houses be surrendered. The devotion of the people is clean gone, their plate and implements sold so that they have nothing left but the lead' (on the roofs).

The Grey Friars, though very poor, do not seem to have made so great lamentations, but the Bishop of Dover, who received the surrender of the four houses in 1539, records that they were 'very poor houses and poor persons,' but 'all meetly leaded.'

Leland notes that in 1538, when he visited the houses, there were many books in the White Friars' Library, but none of any special interest; but in that of the Black Friars there were certain volumes of note, as for example, Turpin's History of Charles the Great (now in the British Museum), Peter of Tarantaise on Virtues and Vices, Epistles of S. Paul and the Fourth Book of the Sentences, and Gorham on S. Luke.

'In no part of the country did the dissolution of the monasteries come with a greater shock in the ruthless sweeping away of the old established order' than in Lincolnshire (*Victoria County History*), where, John Freeman reported to Thomas Cromwell, 'there were more of great houses than in England besides, with thick walls and most part of them vaulted,' so that in the end it was decided to take down the bells and lead on the roofs ('which will bring in 6000 or 7000 marks') and only pull down the roofs, battlements and stairs and leave the walls standing. And thus are preserved to us at least some traces of the architectural glories of mediæval England. The immediate result of this work of destruction was the Pilgrimage of Grace, a rising which began in 1536 at Caister in Lincolnshire. 'On the parts of the insurgents professions of loyalty to the King merge into expressions of hatred and distrust of his confessor, their bishop (Longland), whom they accuse of being the beginning of all this trouble' (*Letters and Papers of Henry VIII*). Boston seems to have taken some part in the insurrection, for it was fined £50 (more than either Lincoln or Stamford), and Guy Kyme and Lord Hussey, both of whom were land-owners in Boston, were executed, the former for actual complicity, the latter for 'sitting on the fence.'

Boston, however, paid up its indemnity, and in 1546 made a tremendous bid for prosperity. In consideration of the payment of the then large sum of £1,646 15s. 4d., Henry VIII granted the town a Charter which incorporated it as a free borough holding directly from the Crown, and conferred on it the whole manor of the Honour of Richmond, with the customs, etc.; the property in Boston of the Religious Houses of Fountains, Durham, Leicester, Barlings, Kirkstead,

Bridlington, Jervant, Swineshead, Thorneholme, Haver-
holme, Nun Ormesby, Alvingham, S. Catherine's at
Lincoln, Bardney, Kyme, Spalding, Stixwold, Louth
Park and Freiston; the property of the White, Austin
and Grey Friars,[1] the Rectory of the Church of S.
Botolph's, the lands of Lord Hussey; the houses belonging to the Gilds and certain private persons, and much
else, and also 'power to assess the inhabitants, as well
unfree as free, with a tax for making a safeguard and
defence of the borough and church there against the
violence of the waters and rage of the sea.' This Charter
was confirmed by Edward VI, but in the meantime the
pillage of the Churches had proceeded, which was what
'the rude commons' had feared in 1536. The church
furniture and goods were sold by the mayor and burgesses apparently between the years 1546 and the final
sale of 1553. The 'petitions' of the mayor, burgesses
and churchwardens in 1552, state that the 'plate and
ornamentes of the said churche dylyveryd by Indenture
by Richard Ogle esquire and other the Kinge majesties
commissioners unto the hands and custodye of the said
churchwardens and by the mare and burgesses of the
said towne' were 'imployede and spent in and uppon
the kynges maiestie affayres and the grate importunate
charges by them susteynede in the reparacion of the
churche Brydge and wharffes there, for the perservacion
of the said towne.' The detailed statement begins (in
order of dates) with the 'repairacon of ye brydge A.o.
1546,' and ends with repairs to the church, bridge and
wharfs in 1550.

Between these dates the bridge was repaired again
twice, and the wharfs twice, which does not speak too

---

[1] The property of the Black Friars was given to Charles Brandon, Duke of
Suffolk.

well for the workmen of that date: £10 was 'expendyde in and aboute the covering and newe laying the steple with lead,' £13 'repayring and amending of the grownde worke of ye churche and of certen wyndowes . . . and ye walles,' and £11 18s. od. for mendying of the south side of the church and leade for the same.' £40 was 'expendyde in and aboute the settyng forth of Sauldeors into norff, to serve the king under the lorde wyllughbye in the tyme of the Commocion there and for gunne powder and other municions for warre.' This was the 1549 rising in Norfolk known as Kett's Rebellion. It seems that each parish in Lincolnshire contributed men or money to the force which was hastily raised in the county and sent against the insurgents under Lord Willoughby of Parham.

The final sale of 'vestmentes copes and other orna-mentes of the church of Boston' was held on the 26th of May, 1553, by commissioners 'assigned by the Kinges highness.' In an inventory of Lincolnshire Church goods of 1553, Boston is noted as having five great bells, one sanctus bell and one chalice weighing 24 ozs., all else presumably had gone (Peacock, *Church Furniture*).

In the meantime, the gilds and their valuables were also going rapidly to their ruin. Although the Charter of Henry VIII stated that 'the aldermen, wardens, or masters and brethren and sisters of all the gilds of Boston were enabled to grant, and the mayor and aldermen to receive all the gild lands and possessions, real and personal, to their use *on condition* that the Cor-poration undertook to maintain and observe all the observations, services, charitable gifts and other ordin-ances of donors to the gilds,' yet it appears that things were in a bad way. Perhaps the members of the gilds felt that in the present distress of the town, it was better to hand over their money for the liquidation of the debt to the Crown, rather than to use it in maintaining the plays of the gilds (always an expensive item), for in 1546, it was determined that 'the Pageants shode not goo in processyon for that yere.' The obits and lights, chaplains, singing clerks, choristers, bedesmen, master of the beggars and schoolmaster, however continue, but in May, 1550, we find the 'Maior' (Mr. Sorsby) riding to London 'for the affaires of the towne,' and by March, 1551, the town had to answer to the 'lorde Admyrall' (Edward Fynes, Lord Clinton) for the lands and possessions of the Corpus Christi Gild, which had been granted to him under the Chantries Act (*Victoria County History*). In June, 1552, it was made known to the Corporation that letters patent of January, 1552, had granted to the Marquis of Northampton (the Lord Chamberlain) 'all the late gilde lands that perteyned to the corporacion, as Our Lady's, S. Peter's, the Trynytie and Saint George's,' and the Corporation, after much discussion decided 'for avoydyng of further damages they thinke and holly agree that . . . they will make and release and surrender' in order that they may 'have this hall and th'arrages with other thynges as may be obtayned,' and in return Lord Northamptonshire granted the burgesses 'all goods and catalls of the gilds' and 'all manner of goods and processyon garments were solde' by order of Henry Hoode, the Mayor, on October 31st, in the Guildhall (*Corporation Records*).

In July, 1553, Lord Northamptonshire was convicted of high treason for supporting Lady Jane Grey in her claim to the throne and his property became forfeit. In October, 1554, 'Thomas Clerk and another' were riding to London about the matter and £20 was given to 'Mr. Cicell for his goodness,' but it was all in vain—

THE SHODFRIARS HALL, BOSTON

much of the property was lost to the Corporation though the Guildhall was saved. Moreover, some of the debt to the Crown was still owing. In 1554–5 it was agreed 'that the house which John Mason dwellith in sholde be solde for payment of £100 to the King and Queenes Maiestie.' For this sum of about £2,000 in modern money Philip and Mary confirmed the Charter of Henry VIII and made over what remained of the gild property 'to the purpose of finding, maintaining and establishing for ever a Free Grammar School in Boston and a fit master or pedagogue to teach, instruct and serve in the said school for the education and instruction of children and youths in grammar and also to find two priests to celebrate divine service in the parish church and four poor inhabitants of the borough to pray there for our good estate while we live and for our souls when we have passed from this light, and for the souls of our ancestors for ever.'

This Grammar School was first carried on in an old building in Wormgate, which had been part of the possessions of the Gild of SS. Peter and Paul; but in 1567, it was agreed that 'ther shal be a new Schole house erected in the Hallgarth' (*Corp. Records*), or Mart Yard, and over the door (now over the porch) was this inscription: 'Ao. 1567 Regine Elizabethe nono Maior et Burgenses de Bostonia uno et eodem consensu puerorum institucionis gracis in piis litteris hanc ædificaverunt Scholam Gulielmo Ganocke stapulæ mercatore, ad tunc maiore existente.'

The school is still in these buildings, with their modern additions, and has reason to be proud of its antiquity, for after all it is the direct descendant of the school maintained by the gilds of Boston's greatest days.

The Corporation appointed the Headmaster and had

F

the school under its immediate care, witness such entries in the Records as 'that a dictionarye shall be bought for the Scollers of the Free Scoole, and the same boke to be tyed to a cheyne and set upon a desk in the scoole, whereunto any scoller may have access as occasion shall serve' (1584), and in 1601 'there shall be boughte at the charges of the Corporation two dictionaries, one greek and one latine and that the schoolmaster for the time being shall see that they be well kepte for the use of the Schoole.' Seventeen years (as may be presumed from the two dates) was not so bad for the life of a dictionary, but after all it was 'tyed to a cheyne and set upon a desk.'

The foundation of the Grammar School is almost the one bright spot in the history of Elizabethan Boston. In consequence of the 'decay of the town' caused by the alteration in the entrance of the river at the Deeps and a lack of sufficient sea marks, Queen Elizabeth, in 1568, granted a Charter of Admiralty, giving the Corporation power to levy certain duties, to take all goods of felons, self-murderers, all wrecks and forfeited goods and the power to punish 'all whoremongers, whores, bawds, panders, and procurers and all other whatsoever living lasciviously and incontinently and also all persons dishonestly and maliciously railing upon every little occasion, which in English, are commonly called scolds.'

In 1568–9 the Maud Foster Drain[1] was cut, in the hope of improving the drainage and carrying off the water, but in 1571 a more than usually high tide and storm of wind and rain devastated the town.[2]

---

[1] So called after the owner of the land through which it was cut.

[2] This is the flood celebrated by Jean Ingelow in her poem, 'High Tide on the Lincolnshire Coast.'

Letters were written from the Corporation to Christopher Audley, an alderman employed about Corporation affairs in London, asking his assistance, and as a result licence was given by Letters Patent empowering the Corporation to purchase 20,000 qrs. of any grain except wheat and export it at 8d. per qr. for five years, 'for the relief and succour of this borough, the inhabitants whereof being greatly impoverished and almost utterly declined, as well by reason of the scarcity of traffic of merchandize, as by the great damage and hurt happened to their port, bridge, wharffs, staithes and seabanks, through the great violence and inundation both of salt and of sea waters.'

At the same time there was much piracy along the coast. Some pirates were captured in 1575 and handed over to Lord Clinton, but doubtless many escaped and continued their depredations.

Boston's troubles continued. It was again visited by plague in 1585, in which year 'the house of Thomas Preston was ordered to be shut up, being supposed to be infected with the plague,' and it was 'agreed that half the collection of the late-visited people should be applied for the relief of the now-visited people,' and sundry sums were given by the Corporation for the relief of those visited by the plague.

The next year there were collections again and a house and two acres were rented for one of 'the visited poor.' In 1587 the Mayor (Thomas Oresby) was directed to keep indoors 'by reason that his house was visited by sickness and not to go abroad in the town till further orders.' In the third year (1588) the plague abated, and 'one Willeman of Holm in Huntingdonshire was sent for, supposed to be skilled in cleaning infected houses.'

It seems that Boston's troubles were so great that it took little active part in the muster against the Spanish Armada (1588), though in 1587, it contributed £6 'for setting forth of the soldiers.'

In 1587 and 1594 bad harvests caused serious dearths and in 1603 the plague returned, so that by 1607, we find the Corporation asking that 'Boston may be put among the decayed towns'; in 1615 relief was asked for 'in respect of provisions levied' (for the King's household) 'upon this town,' and in 1618 a protest 'that the inhabitants of Boston had not usually in former times served any provision for his Majesty of pullings, wax or butter, and that they did not think it convenient that they should be charged with provision of that kind' (Letters to Sir J. Langton, Sir J. Reed, Anthony Irby and others). 1614–15 was a severe winter ending in another great flood, and in 1625 the Fair (S. James') was not held for fear that the plague 'which now is in the City of London and divers places' should be brought again to Boston.

Yet we must not conclude that Boston men spent all their time bewailing their misfortunes and 'the decay' of the town. That, according to their lights, they did their best to combat this 'decay' has been shown, and the lighter side of life is illustrated by chance records. The winter was enlivened by music. 'Edward Astell of Boston, musician, with his several apprentices,' were appointed 'waytes' to the borough. Their duty was 'to play every morning throughout the borough from Michaelmas until Christmas, and from the Twelfth Day (January 6th) until Easter (certain holidays and Fridays excepted) unless reasonable cause be to the contrary. It was therefore agreed by the Mayor and Burgesses that for and towards their paynes and travail in this behalf, every Alderman shall pay to the said Edward yearly so long as he shall continue to be wayte of this borough 4s. by equal payments at Christmas and Easter, and each of the common council 2s. annually in like manner. All other inhabitants to pay yeatly to the said Edward in like manner such sums as they shall be taxed by the Mayor.'

In 1552 and 1553 the 'waytes coates' cost about £1 10s. Boston was not without its dash of fashion also, for we find from the Parish Registers that the art of hair-waving was extensively practised.

But we must turn at the beginning of the seventeenth century, from 'waytes' and hair-waving to the serious business of Puritanism. Dr. Barlow, Bishop of London (1608–13) early declared that the people of Boston were 'a factious people imbued with a Puritan spirit.'

In the Autumn of 1607 certain members of the Puritan congregations of Scrooby, Gainsborough and Standish agreed to meet at Boston, and under the leadership of William Brewster, to make their escape to Holland, where they would be assured that freedom of worship which was denied them in England. This first attempt ended in failure, for the Dutch captain of the ship they had hired betrayed them and they soon found themselves imprisoned under the Guildhall, where the cages in which they were kept are still to be seen. But the magistrates were not inclined to be severe, and, as soon as they were able, they released all except seven, who had to appear at the Assizes at Lincoln, where they were released on their own recognisances. Undeterred by their first repulse, they made a second, and this time successful, attempt the next year.

In the Spring of 1608 they reached Holland, and eleven years later most of them set sail for America and became the founders of New Plymouth Colony, where they inculcated a system of severe morality and sturdy endurance.

Here, then, is the first connection of Boston Lincolnshire with the New World, the second is perhaps even more intimate. In 1612, John Cotton was appointed Vicar of S. Botolph's. He was the son of Roland Cotton, a lawyer of Derby, and was educated at Derby Grammar School and Trinity College, Cambridge. Later he became Fellow and Dean of Magdalen, Cambridge. He married first Elizabeth Horrocks and afterwards Sarah Hawkredd (daughter of Anthony Hawkredd, Mayor of Boston, 1621, and widow of William Storey). Cotton, who was a man of learning and deep piety, was so much respected that, though he could not bring himself to conform to the usage and ceremonies of the Church, he was allowed to carry on his ministrations unmolested for some time, though occasionally Bishops Neile (as strict a disciplinarian as Laud himself) and Montaigne (1614–21) made enquiries into his doings. In answer to one of these Dr. Cotton writes, 'the ceremonies of the ring in marriage, and standing at the creed are generally observed by myself, and other ceremonies of surplices, cross at baptism, kneeling at communion are frequently used by my fellow ministers in our Church. The people on Sabbath and sundry other festival days do very diligently and thoroughly frequent the public prayers of the Church. Sundry do not kneel at communion, which is more from press of numbers.' Bishop Neile's Visitation in 1614 confirms Dr. Cotton's account of the zeal or docility of his congregation.

Service began with the appointed prayers, psalms and lessons, then the 'preacher of the towne bestowed two

hours in a sermon.' More prayers followed, after which
the children were catechized, then followed another
psalm with two hours 'explication'—five hours devotion
in all. A note adds that 'there were as many sleepers as
wakers.' In 1621 a less fortunate Puritan writes 'of all
men I envy Dr. Cotton for he doth nothing in way of
conformity and yet hath his liberty.'

Evidently the influence of John Cotton was para-
mount in Boston.

During his time S. John's church and most of the
chapels in S. Botolph's were destroyed, though the
main fabric was kept in good repair, some of the materials
from S. John's being used for this purpose. We may
gain some idea of what the inside of the church was
like at that time from the orders given in Laud's Archi-
episcopal Visitation for making it 'decent.' The seats
were to be 'rebuilded' so as to leave 'a faire spacious
alley in the middle,' the pavement to be relaid; the
gallery at the east end to be moved to the north; the
inside to be 'whited' and adorned with texts; the Ten
Commandments and the King's Arms to be 'fairly
painted' and put at the east end and the 'room over the
porch to be repaired and made fit for a library in case
any well-disposed person should leave books for the
same' (*Woodward's Register*, Stowe MS.).

The 1614 Visitation of the Lincoln diocese had
reported that there was 'not any forwardness among any
of the ministers to have their children confirmed.' It
was impossible to prohibit 'unauthorized lecturers or
many places would go unserved,' but these lecturers
naturally tended to increase nonconformity, and Archbishop Laud in 1633 had his work cut out to restore
even a semblance of conformity.

In 1630 Dr. Cotton had been disabled by ague, but he

was not a man lightly to resign his ministrations or to leave the place so dear to his heart, and he would doubtless have stuck to his post had he not been cited for nonconformity in 1633 and fined £50 in the Court of High Commission. His many friends, among whom were the Earls of Lincoln and Dorset, counselled him to leave England. He resigned his living in May, 1633, and in July sailed for New England, accompanied by Thomas Hooker, Samuel Stone, Edward Hutchinson and a number of his Boston parishioners. At Trimountain, Massachusetts, he was warmly welcomed, and the guide, counsellor and friend of Lincolnshire Boston became so prominent a leader in his new home that in 1650 the name of the settlement was changed to Boston.

Meanwhile, Boston, Lincolnshire, had not imbibed the teaching and precepts of John Cotton in vain, and when the clouds of civil war were gathering in 1641 a charge of 5s. was made for soldiers 'who went from Boston to Sleaford and 20s. expenses relating to Train Bands.' Next year 'Information was given that his Majesty intended putting garrisons in Lynn, Boston and other sea towns, whereupon it was directed that a general order be drawn to oppose that illegal act' (*Parliamentary Publications*).

The *Perfect Diurnal* of September 19th, 1642, states that 'the Cavaliers were quite cashiered in Lincolnshire,' that 'Boston was well fortified by the inhabitants,' but that the Earl of Lindsey intended shortly to besiege the town, owing it 'a great grudge for having seized some ships laden with corn from Holland and apprehended some officers intending to assist his lordship, but it is believed he will be very roughly entertained.'

The King, indeed, was so displeased at the action of the town that he sent warrants throughout Lincolnshire, making it unlawful for anyone to assist it, 'but,' the *Perfect Diurnal* continues, 'the whole body of that county stand very well affected to Parliament and notwithstanding these warrants the cavaliers dare not enter Boston.'

In 1643, General Fairfax described the town as 'the key of the associated counties," and throughout that year it appears to have been crowded with Puritan soldiers. Between August 20th, 1643, and January 1st, 1644, the burials of 26 soldiers are recorded in the Parish Registers, and they continue at intervals up to March 29th, 1653. One of those marginal notes, which modern vicars would do well to imitate, states that 'the soldiers buried here this year (1643–44) belonged to the Parliamentary army. At this time the Earl of Manchester lay at Boston and was joined by Oliver Cromwell after the defeat of the Earl of Newcastle's troops near Gainsborough.' Cromwell, besides joining Manchester, 'found there assembled Lord Willoughby's detachment and that of Sir Thomas Fairfax, in all making a gallant army' (October 8th, 1643. *Perfect Diurnal*). On this occasion the Puritans bivouacked in the Church and did much harm to it.

The prosperity of Boston as a Puritan centre was, however, short lived. In 1645, a Parliament order was issued to raise £2,000 for the relief of the town, which was to be 'disgarrisoned and the new works slighted,' and this in spite of 'a present of sack and fish to the Earl of Manchester: a supper and present to Colonel Hatcher' (Hacker, one of the regicides) 'entertaining the Scottish Commissioners at the Crown: wine and sugar to Sir Thomas Fairfax.'

But the people continued true to their Puritan principles and showed that Boston was no place for a bishop.

Perhaps they adopted as their war-cry the saying of James I, 'No bishop, no King,' for Dr. Williams, Bishop of Lincoln, writes in 1646 to Nicholas Ferrars, 'You see the times grow high and turbulent and no one knows where the rage and madness of them may end; I am just come from Boston, where I was used very coarsely' (*Life of Nicholas Ferrars.* Wordsworth's *Eccles. Biog.*).

From 1651 Banks Anderson ministered in S. Botolph's, having previously been lecturer under Dr. Tuckney. He was an antipædo-baptist, and was one of the elders summoned by Oliver Cromwell to his Independent Convention in 1658. About the time of his arrival in Boston there was a great witch-hunting campaign on foot. 'Allison's wife' seems to have been the centre of the agitation, and we may easily build up the story from the following items gathered from the Corporation Records, 1649, 'charges for carrying Allison's wife to Lincoln for witchcraft £1 4s.: for sugar and wine at the visiting of Dr. Tuckney (the vicar) 10s. 10d.: Paid Danby and his wife being witness against Allison's wife at Lincoln assizes 18s.: Paid Mr. Stearne for the search of Allison . . . and Sarah Sewally accused for witches £1 4s.' and finally 'Paid to the searcher for her year's salary £2.' There are no more entries about witches, so the 'searcher' evidently did not neglect her work.

After the Civil War there is little to record in the history of Boston. Throughout the seventeenth and eighteenth centuries attempts were made to solve the problem of tides and floods. An Act of Parliament was passed by which Boston was empowered to cut the Witham channel straight and to construct a new sluice.

The Grand Sluice was designed by Langley Edwards and had its foundation carried down twenty feet to a bed of clay. The present Grand Sluice was opened in 1766. To

restore Boston to its mediæval importance was impossible
—the forces of history and of nature were against it—
but the good work done by Dutch engineers in the
eighteenth century, though violently opposed by the
Fen men, secured a very large and fertile tract of land
south-east of Boston, and further works carried out in
1802 reclaimed a still larger area in the east and west,
which led to increased prosperity in Boston and the
building of warehouses on the banks of the Witham
for the storage of corn. Finally, the New Cut was
opened in 1884, and this provided a direct route to
Boston Deeps and a more efficient drainage system, so
that Boston is now a prosperous enough little town.

The grand church, with its dominating 'Stump,'
stands as a witness to the town's former greatness, and
though at first sight it is all too modern, yet a little
probing and a little imagination can conjure up pictures
of mediæval quaintness. Such names as Grey Friars
Lane, White Friars Lane, Shod Friars Lane, Bedesman's
Lane, Corpus Christi Lane, S. Peter's Lane, S. Anne's
Lane and Cross Keys Inn[1] recall the days when the
Friars were a familiar sight in the streets and the Gilds
were an important feature in municipal life. Spain Lane,
Sibsey Lane, Emery Lane, Pulvercroft Lane and Kyme
Tower perpetuate the names of famous Boston families:
Fountain Lane is so called from Fountains Abbey, which
held tenements there; while Wormgate, Bargate and
Barditch suggest the days when a wall and a moat
defended the town.

There are, too, enough old houses standing to give
some idea of what the mediæval streets were like. The
most obvious of these, of course, is the Guildhall and
the so-called Shod Friars Hall south-east of the Market

---

[1] The emblem of S. Peter.

Place; but possibly the most unspoiled bits of old Boston are Spayne Lane, with its old store houses and Duckfield Lane (so-called from the Duchefielde family of the fourteenth and fifteenth centuries), where the lower part of Messrs. Hurst's warehouse is all that is left of Gysor's Hall, held by John de Gysor (Mayor of London in 1245), for which he paid to the Honour of Richmond one pair of hose and one pair of gilt spurs.

John Ray's description of Boston, written in 1662, holds good in the main to-day. 'It is truly observed by Camden,' he says, 'that in Holland in Lincolnshire and generally in all the Fen countries the churches are very fair and built of stone, though the country thereabouts for many miles scarcely affords a pebble. July 27 and 28 we lodged at Boston. The town for that country is large, populous and hath a good trade. The Steeple for a tower, the tallest that ever I saw. The church is fair and great, standing in a level country it may be seen for many miles, and is also a sea-mark, from the ground to the highest top the ascent is 364 steps. The lead lanthorn (as they call it) is uncovered, and raised at the leads to a very considerable height, viz., 79ft. There is a kind of exchange, which they call the Mart-Yard (by Camden called the Gild) and a Free-School and some other buildings which we noticed' (*Itinerary*).

CHAPTER V

THE CHURCH OF S. BOTOLPH

THE magnificent Church of S. Botolph, one of the noblest religious edifices in England, is justly celebrated far and wide, not only by reason of its imposing appearance, but also for its historic associations and the piety of which it is the embodiment. Standing out boldly, with its east end projecting into the Market Place, and its great west tower rising immediately from the bank of the river Witham, it is the crowning glory of the old town of Boston.

The most beautiful feature of the whole building is its tremendous tower, a particularly fine specimen of Gothic art, raised in the perpendicular style, and in height exceeding any English Cathedral tower. The Clock Tower of Westminster is near akin in design and effect, but in grandeur its only serious rival is to be found in the noble Cathedral of Rouen. For six centuries the tower of the church of S. Botolph has been a distinctive feature from land and sea for a radius of forty miles, and, crowned with its beacon lantern, has stood like a guardian over the Fens.

Locally the church is known as 'Boston Stump'—a name expressive of the sturdy solidity of the front it offers to all the winds of heaven. It is the largest and most imposing parish church in England, for in area it is exceeded only by that of S. Nicholas, Yarmouth. The tower of S. Botolph, however, rises much higher, and it is this very loftiness, together with its nobility and beauty of design, and its graceful proportions, mellowed by the charm of centuries, which makes this majestic structure the admiration of all visitors.

The present church is the third to occupy this site, the first being the monastery of S. Botolph, the hermit Abbot and founder of Boston. Not much is known of this saint, the friend of boatmen, though the Venerable Bede says he was born of a gentle Saxon family and was educated in Belgium, where he acquired a great reputation for piety and learning. In the same monastery were the two sisters of Ethelmund, King of East Anglia, who had also been sent to profit by the learning of the day and to receive religious instruction. Knowing that S. Botolph wished to return to his home land, these royal sisters gave him a recommendation to their brother, from whom he afterwards begged permission to build a monastery in some desolate place where no man dwelt. The king willingly gave him the choice of his domain, and the wilderness he selected was an island in the fens and swamps beside the river Witham, known as Icanho (Ox Island), which as yet had not been inhabited. Here he built his monastery and settled with his monks, whom he instructed in the Faith which he had learnt abroad, and gained the love of all by his humility and holiness. He became famous also for his gift of prophecy, since he often foretold events which afterwards happened as he had predicted. So under his care in this dreary fen this colony of monks increased, and S. Botolph became the founder in England of the Benedictine Order. But in 680 he died, and was buried in the monastery which he had built. Here his sacred relics remained until 870, when all holy places were laid waste by the Danes, and this monastery was destroyed. Then, we are told, the 'relics of the saint were safely translated, part to Ely and part to Thorney,' but his memory is preserved by the annual festival on June 17th, and sixty of our oldest churches are dedicated in his honour. The remains of the building, however, were eventually restored, and round this nucleus other dwellings sprang up, till later S. Botolph's ton became a very important town.

At the time of the Norman Conquest a small monastery here still preserved the name of S. Botolph, and history records that lands around Boston were granted by the Conqueror to Alan Rufus, Earl of Brittany, and nephew of William the Conqueror. Shortly before his death in 1090, Alan obtained also the ordination of the rectory of Boston, which he afterwards endowed, giving the patronage to the church of the Benedictine Abbey of S. Mary at York.

The monks apparently rebuilt the church and replaced a wooden structure by a small stone building, for during the restoration in 1851–3, the foundations of this church were exposed, showing that it consisted of a nave, aisles, chancel and tower, with the floor four feet below the present one. These discoveries bear out the records of Leland, for according to him Boston had another church at this time, called S. John's. This seems to have been the chief parish church, for the Mother Church, which was connected with S. Mary's at York, was smaller and stood on the site of the present one.

The entry in Domesday Book also shows that S. Botolph's was not a separate parish, but that Boston then formed part of the parish of Skirbeck. By the twelfth century, however, the town had become very rich and prosperous, owing to its being at the same time a thriving seaport and a great centre for the wool trade. For many years it was the second port in the kingdom, and in the latter part of the thirteenth century it became the most important, and paid custom duties amounting to one third more than those of London.

Since Boston was now a town of the very first rank, it is not surprising to find that four Orders of Friars were established within its limits—Dominicans, Franciscans, Austins and Carmelites, whose work and preaching brought about a great religious revival. This keen enthusiasm found its expression in the desire to build a church, which in beauty and design should be second to none in all the Christendom of that time—a desire which was realised in the magnificent church of to-day.

The digging for the foundation was begun on Monday in Holy Week in 1309, and on the Monday after the Feast of S. John Baptist, Dame Margery Tilney laid the foundation stone; and on it placed £5. She was assisted at the ceremony by Sir John Truesdale, the rector of Boston, and Richard Stephenson, a merchant of Boston, who also contributed £5 each; so that the building of this great church began with the sum of £15. The present church appears to have been erected over the old one, which was left standing during its construction; but the tower, which is an addition, was built 100 years later. Tradition says that the foundation of the steeple was laid on wool sacks. Wool, indeed, contributed most to the wealth of the town, so that the money needed for laying the foundation, without a doubt, was raised chiefly from trade in this commodity. It is certain that, owing to the treacherous nature of the banks of the tidal river, the foundation was laid with the greatest care.

The original design shows that the church consisted

BOSTON DOCKS

of a nave, with aisles each of seven bays, and fourteen clerestory windows on each side of the nave; the chancel of three bays; and a south porch with a chapel on either side, the one on the east being now destroyed. All this is decorated work, which was the prevailing style when the building was begun, but as the church was nearing completion, a change of style was adopted, as is shown by the introduction of the perpendicular in several places; while the tower, which was raised a century later, is a fine specimen of pure perpendicular work. In a part of the parapet of the north aisle there is also incorporated the rich Tudor Gothic of the time of Henry VIII.

Leland says that the Tilney family were the chief benefactors of this building, and he states that 'the chiefe paroche chirche was at St. John's, where yet is a chirche for the toune. St. Botolph's was but a chapel to it, but it is now so risen and adornid, that it is the chiefiest of the toune, and for a paroche chirche, the best and fayrest of al Lincolnshire, and served so with singging and that of cunning men as no paroche is in al England.'

During the erection of the tower some alterations were made. The two turrets which had formerly flanked the west front were retained and converted into stair turrets leading to the tower, and the west window of the nave was removed to its present position. In the same period, the chancel was extended eastwards by the addition of two bays, the nave was also repaired and reroofed, and a chamber over the porch erected. Two chapels were also added, one at the east end of each aisle, thus forming very low transepts. The sacristy along the south side of the chancel was built, and a small chapel erected west of the north door.

G

Finally, in 1460, the square tower was crowned by the erection of the beautiful octagonal lantern, the whole church, therefore, took about 150 years in building, which was carried forward through the reigns of six different sovereigns. What other additions were intended to be made, we do not know; but from the putlog holes still remaining in the lantern, and the stone springers in the interior of the belfry, we may conclude that the work was hastily finished off and was never regarded as being actually completed.

Perhaps here we may allow our thoughts to take us back to those pre-Reformation days when four orders of Friars and a number of guilds were established in the town. S. Botolph's, with its many chapels, was a great centre of all religious activities, and we can quite imagine the impressive services conducted on days of high festivals in a church so beautifully decorated and admirably constructed for ritual and ceremony. At the Reformation, however, the church suffered serious damage, the screens were broken, the statues and ornaments were thrown down, and all the stained glass windows, together with the plate, vestments, needlework and other decorations were destroyed. Further outrages occurred in 1626, when the chapel on the east side of the porch was demolished. During the Cromwellian campaign the church for a time served as a cavalry stable, and the iron rings, to which the horses were tied, remained fastened to the pillars until 1851. In the west wall, too, pits may still be seen which were made by the soldiers in their musketry practice. Again, a few years later, another outrage occurred, when the figure of S. Botolph, as a mitred abbot holding a model of the church in his hand, was broken down by a Puritan, named Atherton Hough, a churchwarden, because he considered that it resembled the Pope. He subsequently fled with John Cotton, the vicar, to Massachusetts. The statue was restored, but some years later it was struck by lightning, again repaired, and raised to its present lofty position on the tower. At this time most of the brasses were torn away, but in Haines' Book of Monumental Brasses, published in 1861, he mentions twelve as existing at that date. There were also loose brasses kept in the library at that time, and in the British Museum there are notices of some that are now lost.

The chapels and appendages of the church appeared to have served various purposes, both religious and secular. The Porch, as in many other churches, was often used for the performance of several types of religious cere-monies, such as Baptism, and the first part of the Marriage Service. Business relating to the poor was also trans-acted here, and many differences of the Hundred were also legally settled here just as in the King's Court.

The chapels were used mainly by the different gilds (of which there were fifteen in the town), but the chapel on the west of the porch was also used as a school, which was founded by John Laughton in 1707. It is now called the Cotton Chapel, in memory of John Cotton, a former vicar, who for pious reasons left Boston and joined the Pilgrim Fathers in Massachusetts in 1633. The room above the porch, or the Parvise, which now serves as a library, was used for several purposes, but generally as a school, for we are told that, until 1635, it was used for 'teaching of petty scholars,' and then at the request of Anthony Tuckney, vicar of Boston, it was ordered by the Archbishop of Canterbury to be fitted up as a library.

On reference to historical records, we see that various grants were made to the rectory of Boston, for in the

Patent Rolls in the Tower, entries were made in the years 1321, 1342 and again in 1409, showing that grants were issued, and the Charter Rolls also show that a licence was granted to give the parson of S. Botolph's certain lands to be added to the burial ground (P. Thompson).

History also records that the Abbot and Convent of S. Mary at York possessed the patronage of the living until 1486, when it was given by them to the King because they had been released from certain dues to the Duchy of Lancaster. The King afterwards exchanged it with the Prior of S. John of Jerusalem, who was then Sir John Weston, for certain lands in Leicestershire which are known as Beaumonds Lees. The Prior petitioned for the Rectory also, and it remained in the possession of this Order until the Dissolution of the Monasteries. The living was then formed into a vicarage, and the rector's house near the church became the residence of the vicar. The advowson was given to the Mayor and Corporation, but in 1835 it passed to the Bishop of the Diocese.

By the fifteenth century the trade of Boston began to decline, and in the days of Elizabeth the port seems to have been brought nearly to ruin, probably by the silting up of the river Witham and the shifting sands of the Wash.

On the restoration of the King in 1660, however, the church was again used for its rightful purpose and some repairs were made to the fabric; but Boston was then very Puritan in tone, and had become so thoroughly impoverished that really very little was done. Throughout the seventeenth century little attention was given to the preservation of the building, so that it was kept barely in a fit condition for use, though necessary repairs were made to the chancel in 1663, 1666 and in 1674. Early in the eighteenth century the chapel on the north side of the Chancel, the Sacristy and Taylor's Hall, were destroyed. In 1742, however, a great improvement was made by the gift from Mr. John Parish, of a public-house called the Ostrich. This inn, together with a few small cottages near the church, was cleared away, and the land on which they formerly stood was added to the churchyard which now forms the church close. In 1840 a genuine restoration began, and further extensive repairs were carried out in 1851-3 at a cost of £10,996, when Sir G. G. Scott acted as consulting architect. Other minor improvements have been made more recently, and in 1928 the roof was found to be in urgent need of repair owing to the ravages of the death-watch beetle. So in the confident hope that the sum of £30,000 required for the complete restoration would be forthcoming, this great work was started on Monday in Holy Week in the year 1929, the 620th anniversary of the day when the first foundation stone was laid.

THE EXTERIOR OF THE CHURCH

As one approaches the church from the Market Place one passes through the well-kept Close, and while following the path to the porch, obtains a general view of the east end, south aisle, porch and tower; but the immense size of the structure as a whole and the graceful dignity of the magnificent tower at once rivet the attention.

Continuing the walk round the west end and along the north aisle it will be seen that the general plan is quite an ordinary one, for the church consists of a Chancel with a small chapel on the north, now used as the organ chamber; a Nave with the north and south aisles; the Porch with its upper room now used as a library; the Founders or Cotton Chapel adjoining the west wall of the porch; the small engine room; and the great Tower Steeple, forming the west end of the church.

It will be noticed, of course, that the architecture gives evidence of the period when the church was built and when additions were made. The nave and the walls of the north and south aisles present examples of decorated work, the prevailing style when the foundations were laid; but as the building extended into the perpendicular period, this style is introduced in several places, while the tower is a specimen of pure perpendicular work. Also a glimpse of the rich Tudor Gothic of the time of Henry VIII may be seen in the parapet of the north aisle. The church is not lavishly ornamented, but sufficiently so for architectural effect, and it must be remembered, that because of the many religious outrages, it has been stripped of nearly all its statuary, and, with one exception, the many chapels formerly attached to it.

The visitor should now make a closer inspection, starting at the east end of the chancel. This contains a well-proportioned window of seven lights and flowing modern (1852) tracery. The buttresses are interesting, for the lower portions are decorated work, while the upper are in the light perpendicular style, since during the perpendicular period, the original east end was rebuilt on new foundations two bays further east.

The two styles of architecture will be seen again on the south side of the chancel, which has five bays, each containing a window with four lights, for the three west windows are the original decorated ones, while the other two were added during the perpendicular period. The whole of the parapet and pinnacles are perpendicular work. On this side, too, may be seen the Priest's door, opening into the Sacristy, which formerly stood in front of the two west windows and was removed in 1725. At the same time an adjoining building, called the Taylor's Hall, was taken down.

The south aisle also has five bays, each with a window of four lights, with decorated tracery varying alternately in design in each window, and between the bays are buttresses with pediments ornamented with gargoyle figures. The buttress near the porch has a niche with a crocketed pediment and canopy, now sadly mutilated. East of this was formerly a broad and low opening with a pointed arch richly moulded, and under the window next to the porch there appears to have been another opening to a chapel now removed. The east end window of the south aisle has five lights with perpendicular cinquefoiled tracery. The parapet above the window has open quatrefoiled circles, while the southeast buttresses are surmounted by an elaborate square pinnacle which has panelled sides with canopies and niches for statues, and terminates in a finialed and crocketed cone.

The south porch and chapel are also along this side. The architecture of the porch is interesting, since it is two stories in height, the upper room being a specimen of perpendicular style, while the lower part, including the doorway inside, is a fine example of decorated work. The history of the door itself carries us back to the fourteenth century, and the plain cross cut in the stone on the eastern side of the doorway, is one of the twelve crosses marked by the bishop when the church was dedicated. The staircase seen in the east wall leads to the upper room which is now used as a library. Until 1635, this room was used for several purposes, generally as a school, 'for the teaching of petty scholars,' but at the request of Anthony Tuckney, vicar of Boston, it was ordained by the Archbishop of Canterbury on his visit that year, that it should be furnished as a library. It now contains many rare and valuable books and publications, including *King Edward VI's Liturgy*, the *Homilies*, *Bede*, and a copy of Clement Cotton's *Concordance*, 2nd edition, printed in London in 1635. The south wall of the library has a handsome window with five lights, and the east wall contains four square-headed windows. The lower part of the buttresses contain very elaborate canopied niches, and the gable terminates in a beautiful large stone cross. The south-east pinnacle was restored in 1904.

The Chapel, known as the Cotton Chapel, adjoins the west wall of the porch and was built during the decorated period. The south wall is three bays in length and has three windows of three lights each and quatrefoiled tracery. The buttresses between the windows have crocketed pediments, and above is a plain parapet. The west wall of the chapel has a window of four lights and perpendicular tracery, and terminates in a gable flanked by buttresses. The chapel was formerly used as a school, which was founded by Mr. John Laughton in 1707, but now it is reserved for private meditation.

It will be noticed that the west end of the south aisle has a window corresponding to that in the east end, with five lights and perpendicular tracery.

The south wall of the nave clerestory has twice as many bays as the aisle, and is pierced with fourteen windows of two lights, with decorated tracery of two designs used alternately. The buttresses contain canopies for statues, though most of these graceful figures have been removed or mutilated.

The tower, although built a century later, is in perfect harmony with the rest of the building. It shows four stages, and reaches to a height of 270 feet. The first stage, which is as high as the roof of the nave, contains the west door, the great west window, and two other windows on the north and south sides. This stage is supported by great shafted buttresses with graceful statues adding to the effect. The second story is the most beautiful part of the whole, and contains twin windows in each of the four walls. The third stage, which forms the bell chamber, is beautifully designed with pinnacles and battlements, and is lighted by four large perpendicular windows. At the base of this story an external gallery, reached by an inner staircase, is constructed round the tower. The fourth stage is the wonderful octagonal lantern which rests on the square tower and is supported by four great flying buttresses. The lantern is exceedingly beautiful, and is very graceful and light in construction. Each face contains a window of two lights divided by transoms into three parts, so that the lantern gives in design and treatment a similar impression to that of the second story. The parapet has richly ornamented gables of open tracery work, and above this rise eight pinnacles with their gilded vanes.

The figure of S. Botolph, as a mitred abbot, may be seen on a tall narrow turret which rises out of one of the six great corner buttresses.

The west door which opens into the tower is part of the original door which gave entrance to the west end of the nave before the tower was built; though much mutilated, it reveals beautiful work.

The north aisle has seven windows with tracery similar to those of the south aisle. The buttresses between them are in two stages, with richly carved pediments having delicate crockets and finials, though these are much decayed. The curved heads at the top of the window arches are uncommon and worthy of note.

The west wall of the north aisle has a window resembling that of the south aisle. It has a plain parapet, but at the corner is an octangular turret with canopies, pediments, and niches, with a handsome crocketed pinnacle. It appears to have had three tiers of statues, and those remaining show very delicate workmanship.

The north door, without a porch, opens immediately into the nave, and has a pointed arch. Old drawings of the church show that a small chamber, used as a charnel house, formerly stood west of this door.

The east end of this aisle is pierced by a window similar to that in the south aisle, and above is a cornice with bosses and heads. The parapet, of the late perpendicular period of Henry VIII, is a piece of remarkably rich and delicate workmanship. The tracery is exceedingly well sculptured, and though it has been compared with that in the Henry VII Chapel at Westminster, it is acknowledged to have no superior or even equal; and the adjoining pinnacle is of similar beauty. The square turrets seen at the north-east corner have canopies and niches containing figures, but during the Puritan outrages these were badly mutilated.

A chapel formerly stood at the end of this aisle, but was removed in 1717. Now a small building joined to the nave, aisle, and chancel contains the stairs leading to the organ loft, which is lighted by a square-headed window.

It will be noticed that the north clerestory corresponds to that of the south, though it has more statues, and the north side of the chancel resembles the south side, but the north-east window is partly blocked. This work was done during the Middle Ages in order to give support to the wall.

The Interior of the Church

As one enters the church it is possible to obtain a view of almost the whole of the interior at once, owing to the absence of transepts and chapels. At the same time the lack of ornamentation and colour is noticeable, for all the original decorations, stained glass, carved screens and other ornaments, which are usually found in decorated churches, have been destroyed. While the interior view of the church rouses a feeling of awe and devotion, there is also a consciousness of desolate bareness.

The massive south door is an object of attraction, with its elaborate oak carving of two different designs of the decorated period, and is one of the best specimens of its date. The noble proportions of the church may be best appreciated if one stands by the great west door and looks towards the High Altar, for the length of the church extends over 300 feet, and the interior breadth is nearly 100 feet, while the height of the groined ceiling in the tower above him exceeds 150 feet. The width of the aisles, too, is a very striking feature, as is the height of the nave with its twelve tall clustered pillars, and also the extensive chancel; a fit place, indeed, for those stately services of pre-Reformation days, when the Latin tongue was heard in church, and art and music lent their aid to the service of God.

It is interesting to note that various parts of the

building correspond to various periods of time. There are twelve pillars in the nave and twelve months in the year, fifty-two windows in the building and fifty-two weeks in a year, 365 steps up the tower and 365 days in the year, seven doors in the church and seven days in the week, twenty-four steps leading to the library and twenty-four hours in the day, and finally, sixty steps ascending to the roof and sixty minutes in the hour.

The original flat panelled ceiling of the nave with paintings of scriptural and historical subjects, which was supported by fifteen large oak beams stretching across from north to south, and resting on a carved cornice between each pair of clerestory windows, was replaced by a groined wooden structure in 1781. The original ceilings of the aisles were similar and were also removed. In 1929 these vaulted roofs became unsafe owing to the ravages of the death-watch beetle, and were again replaced with flat painted oak panels following the original design.

It will be seen that the first stage of the tower is open to the church, and has a magnificent modern stone vaulting at the height of 156 feet from the floor, which is said to be the highest stone roof in the world. By the aid of a mirror an inspection of the details of this wonderful work of art can be made. The great central boss, which before being carved weighed six tons, represents the Agnus Dei, and the other large bosses represent the four living creatures and four angels with the words 'O Lamb of God.' The surrounding smaller ones are carved as foliage. The space under the tower is now used as the vestry. The arch between it and the nave was originally filled by the west window, and the position of the sill can be seen from the nave, for since the tower was a later addition, this was formerly the outer west end of the church. The doors on each side of the arch open to the spiral staircases which lead to the roof and tower. On the door of the north staircase is a curious bronze handle, circular in shape, and formed by two lizards held in the mouth of a lion. Permission to ascend the tower is granted on payment of a small fee, and the climb up the 365 steps will amply repay the visitor for his efforts. On a clear day he will obtain an extensive view over the low flat country, and be able to see Tattershall Castle which is fourteen miles distant, Lincoln Cathedral thirty-two miles to the north, and the Norfolk coast which lies on the horizon beyond the Wash. The staircases lead in stages to the top, the first stage reaches to the first outside gallery and also opens into the belfry containing the famous bells. The second stage reaches to the next gallery, and if his energy permits, the visitor may ascend the lantern from the top of the tower.

The bells of S. Botolph's can be heard for miles over this low district. The first mention of the bells was in 1553, when there were 'five great bells in the tower and a Sanctus bell.' Then in 1709 the old clock bell, weighing over 4,000 lbs., was recast, and three new bells were made from the metal. At the present time there are twelve bells, and until recently they were chimed at intervals of three hours from 9 a.m. to 9 p.m. The eighth bell bears this curious inscription:

> 'All men that heare my mourniful sound
> Repent before you lie in ground.'
>
> G+O. 1617.

On returning to the nave one will notice that it is separated from each aisle by six clustered pillars with plain moulded bases and caps. These also support seven pointed arches and the wall of the clerestory. Many of the windows are fitted with plain glass, and cast a cold glare in contrast to the more subdued light which passes through those filled with coloured glass.

The south aisle contains five windows, the most westward one being plain, while the remaining four are furnished with stained glass. The first one was presented by Anne Bowman in 1926, in memory of her brothers, John Thomas Bradley and George Henry Bradley. The next was presented by Mrs. Elizabeth Tilson Bradshaw in 1895. The glass is by Powell and represents the Baptism of Christ, S. Peter preaching, the martyrdom of S. Stephen, and figures of S. John the Baptist, S. Paul, S. Peter and S. Stephen. The third coloured window, which is the largest in this aisle, has stained glass designed by Hardman, and represents some of the Parables of our Lord. It was inserted in 1876 in memory of Samuel Henry Jebb and Frances his wife.

The window occupying the last bay of the south aisle also has glass by Hardman and is a memorial to Thomas Garfit, M.P. for Boston, who died in 1883. The design represents the Conversion of S. Paul, his trial before Festus, and four miracles from the Acts of the Apostles. The glass in the east window of this aisle, which is also the window of the Lady Chapel, is the most beautiful in the church. It is a memorial to Alice Scrivener, who died in 1889, and represents the Marys, the design being the work of the artist Kempe. In it are seen the Blessed Virgin Mary with the infant Saviour, S. Anne with the infant S. Mary, S. Mary of Bethany, S. Mary Magdalene and S. Elizabeth with the infant S. John, and below are Angels with musical instruments.

It will be noticed that the wall of the south aisle contains the door opening on the staircase to the library, as well as five recesses or doorways. The first doorway, which is now blocked, formerly opened into a chapel no longer in existence, and the first of the three recesses also probably opened into a chapel. The second contains the alabaster figure of a lady on a tomb of black marble which is carved with quatrefoiled circles enclosing shields; the central one may have represented the Tilney arms. The third recess contains an alabaster tomb on which lies the figure of a knight in armour. The Maltese cross round his neck indicates his order of S. John of Jerusalem. It will be seen that the tomb is divided into four panels, on each of which is carved an angel bearing a shield. These tombs, dating from the fourteenth century, were formerly in the church of S. John, but in 1626, they were removed to S. Botolph's, and were placed in these recesses in the eighteenth century. A little further east is a blocked doorway which formerly gave entrance to a stairway leading to the rood loft of S. Mary's Chapel. Over the doorway is a hatchment, and above that is an opening on to the loft which was supported by a screen. The loft crossed the aisle to the opposite pillar, and a similar screen continued along the two bays separating the chapel from the nave. This chapel was refurnished and brought into use as a memorial to the Bostonians who fell in the Great War, 1914–8. The next sepulchral recess contains a stone coffin with a floriated cross carved on the lid, and just above are two beautifully carved niches for statues, the one on the west containing the figure of S. Gregory, with a tablet in memory of a former organist of this church.

The last bay of this aisle was probably raised to form the altar platform of the chapel. Below the window are three stone sedilia separated from each other by two clustered marble pillars. East of these were formerly an

aumbry, and a piscina now blocked, for prior to the
Reformation there was a private chapel or altar here.

Various memorials appear on the wall of the south
aisle. West of the door is a large hatchment bearing
the royal arms of Charles II, and near the door are two
marble tablets, the upper one in memory of Frances
Clerk of Peterborough, who died in 1761; and the lower
in memory of John Wayet, who died in 1784, and Mary
his wife, John Wayet, their son, and Anne his wife.
Near these is also another memorial in wood in memory
of Richard Smith, who died in 1626. East of the south
door, in the first blocked doorway, is a brass tablet
inscribed in Latin to the memory of Henry Hallam, the
historian; and on either side of the first sepulchral recess
is a hatchment, bearing the arms of Smith, Kyme, and
Carr in the one case, and in the other the arms of Carr,
with quarterings, two of which are obscure. Below
these is a marble tablet to the memory of John Skynner
Baily, who died in 1838, and Hannah his wife, who died
in 1842; and over the stone coffin in the next recess are
three tablets, a brass one with the coat of arms, in
memory of John Townley, Controller of the Port and
Alderman of Boston, who died in 1588, and Joanna his
wife; a copper tablet with an inscription in memory of
Robert Wilby, Mayor and Alderman, who died in 1791;
and another brass tablet with a coat of arms and Latin
inscription in memory of Pishy Thompson, the historian
of Boston, who died in 1862. Near this is another tablet
in brass, recently added in memory of Meaburn Staniland and Geoffrey Staniland. Above this recess may be
seen a tablet in marble in memory of John Parish, who
gave the land on which stood the old Ostrich Inn, to be
added to the church close. On the blocked doorway
which led to the rood loft is a plate bearing a shield, and

THE CHURCH OF S. NICHOLAS, SKIRBECK

below that is another in memory of Richard Belfe, of
Hough, who died in 1571.

On the east wall of this aisle is a marble tablet in
memory of William Clayton who died in 1817, and
below this is a gravestone with a coat of arms in memory
of Nathaniel Kone, who died in 1654. Above the
east window is an old and interesting stone tablet in a
stone frame, representing a skeleton holding a scroll in
memory of William Whitley and Mary his wife, given
by their son in 1730 and beneath this is a brass
in memory of Boron Iren who died in the south. Above
Wm. Frederick Winfield Harwood and William
Frederick Long.

The south aisle is similar in structure to the north
aisle. The two eastern bays originally formed the
chapel of SS. Peter and Paul which was probably
screened off as with the chapel of S. Mary at the east
end of the north aisle. Formerly the door opened from
this chapel to another chapel on the north, which has
been removed, but now in place are the steps
leading to the organ chamber.

All the windows of this aisle are filled with plain glass
except the east window and the one over the north
door. The glass in the east window is in memory
and is a memorial to Samuel De Bary Leigh, who died
in 1918. In it are represented the types saints David,
Samuel, Simeon, Zacharias, and Enoch, below the two figures.
The window over the south door is also the work of
Hardman and is in memory [of] Stephen Leigh and
Hannah his wife, it illustrates the Dedication of
Solomon's Temple, the showing Solomon, the Dedication of Christ in the Temple, and the Dedication and
Finance. This window also has very beautiful colours
in which may be seen the figure [?].

below that is another in memory of Richard Bolle of Hough, who died in 1591.

On the east wall of this aisle is a marble tablet in memory of William Chapman who died in 1817, and below this is a brass one with a coat of arms in memory of Nightingale Kyme who died in 1814. Under the east window is an old and interesting brass tablet in a stone frame, representing a skeleton holding a scroll in memory of William Dingley and Mary his wife, given by their son in 1626; and on each side of this is a brass in memory of Boston men who fell in the South African War, Frederick Wingfield Harwood and William Frederick Long.

The north aisle is similar in structure to the south aisle. The two eastern bays originally formed the chapel of SS. Peter and Paul, which was probably screened off as with the chapel of S. Mary at the east end of the south aisle. Formerly the door opened from this chapel to another chapel on the north, which has been removed, but now it gives access to the staircase leading to the organ chamber.

All the windows of this aisle are fitted with plain glass except the east window and the one over the north door. The glass in the east window is by Hardman, and is a memorial to Samuel Richard Fydell, who died in 1868. In it are represented five aged saints: David, Samuel, Simeon, Zacharias, and S. John the Evangelist. The window over the north door is also the work of Hardman, and is a memorial to John Skynner Baily and Hannah his wife. It illustrates the Dedication of Solomon's Temple, Eli blessing Hannah, the Presentation of Christ in the Temple, and the Pharisee and the Publican. This window also has very beautiful tracery in which may be seen the Agnus Dei.

H

The north wall has three sepulchral recesses. The most easterly one contains the broken lid of an ancient stone coffin, and the other two are empty. There are also three hatchments.

The walls of the north aisle bear a number of interesting memorials. On the north side of the chancel arch is a tablet in a marble frame, in memory of Thomas Basil Wood and Charles Sinclair Wood, both officers killed in the Great War. Nearly all the memorials in the chapel of SS. Peter and Paul refer to members of the Fydell family, once distinguished in the commercial life of the town. The two tablets in the hatchments on each side of the window are in memory of Elizabeth, the wife of Samuel Fydell, who died in 1816, and Elizabeth, the widow of Richard Fydell, who died in 1783. Near these is an alabaster tablet with a Latin inscription, in memory of Peter Baldwer, who died in 1691, and on the wall west of the window is an elaborate memorial representing a bust and coat of arms, to Richard Fydell, who died in 1780. Next to it is another in memory of Thomas Fydell, who died in 1802, and of Elizabeth his wife, who died in 1813. A tablet in memory of Henry Butler Pacey, who died in 1785, is also on this wall, and close to the north door is a small tablet in memory of the Rev. Bartholomew Goe, Vicar of Boston, who died in 1838. Just above is a bust of Herbert Ingram, which is the work of Westmacott.

Near here, too, will be seen an Italian picture of the Holy Family, presented by Mr. G. E. Hackford, and also copies of three of Rubens' pictures by P. Mequignon, which were presented by William Smith. They represent the Visitation, the Crucifixion, and the Presentation in the Temple. They are arranged as a triptych, and formed the reredos from 1799 to 1850. On each side of the west window of this aisle is a tablet, one in memory of Charlotte Wilford, who died in 1836, and the other of Job Phillips, who died in 1850.

On the north side of the great arch is a renaissance monument to the memory of John Wood, and another on the south to John Boult, both of whom died in 1702. Three other tablets may be seen under the west window of the south aisle, in memory of Henry Gee, who died in 1845, Martha Fitzwilliam, his wife, who died in 1836, and of the Rev. John Wayet, who died in 1825.

Perhaps the oldest and most interesting monument in the church is to be found on the floor of the north aisle in the form of a black marble slab. It was unearthed in the eighteenth century on the site of the church of the Franciscan Friary, and after forming part of the wall of a cottage, it was placed in the church in 1897. Incised on it is a figure standing under a canopy with a dog at the feet and the hands joined in prayer. In the corners are the emblems of the four Evangelists, and round the margin is the following inscription in Latin: 'Here lies Wisselus surnamed Smalenburg, citizen and merchant of Munster who died on the Friday after the Nativity of the Blessed Virgin Mary 1340. May his soul rest in peace.'

Another peculiar type of monument may be seen on the pavement near the font, though there are others of the same kind in other parts of the church. On slabs of black marble are chiselled the outline of the deceased with the head and hands inlaid in white marble. Since the outlines have been worn away, these monuments present a weird appearance to-day. A brass in memory of John Tooley, who died in 1686, may be seen near the font; two other brasses still remain on the floor in the sanctuary, and a small one of later date at the east end of the nave.

The old vestry chest dates back over two hundred years, and stands under the west window.

The chapel, known as the Cotton Chapel, adjoins the west wall of the porch, and is separated from the south aisle by two arches. The lower part of these arches is fitted with an oak screen which was erected in 1895. There is an external door in the south wall and a blocked doorway in the north wall formerly opening into the sacristy which has now been removed. This chapel was originally known as Founder's Chapel, but its dedication is uncertain, and it was used for a school founded by Mr. John Laughton in 1707. Later it served as the vestry and contained the old chest and several old books. It is now known as the Chapel, or the Cotton Chapel, having been restored and refurnished in 1856 mainly by the generosity of citizens of Boston, U.S.A., in memory of John Cotton, a former vicar, and an early settler in Massachusetts.

The three south windows, with their reticulated tracery, are fitted with stained glass. One is by Hardman in memory of James Armitage Hartley, who died in 1877, and represents Moses, Saul and Gamaliel, and Nehemiah; the second is by Ballantine and in memory of John Laughton, who founded the school formerly held in this chapel. The glass represents Christ with the Doctors, Christ placing a little Child among His Disciples, and Christ blessing little Children. The third window is also the work of Hardman and represents Aquila, Priscilla, and Apollos, and is a memorial to William Gane and Elizabeth Sofia his wife. The west window of the chapel has perpendicular tracery, and the ceiling of plain oak dates back to the same period. It will be noticed that the stone corbels are carved with the coat of arms of some of the first New England settlers.

The altar, which is a memorial to Frances Anne
Lawrence, stands in an arched recess at the east end,
and the reredos is a carved oak triptych which was
presented by Elizabeth and Marianne Storr. A large
recess will be noticed near the altar, and the remains of
a piscina which has been stripped of all its carving.

There are several memorials in the chapel. One is a
brass tablet in a carved stone frame in memory of John
Cotton, a former vicar who found a new home in
America, and is inscribed by Mr. Everett, an American
and descendant. Over the door is another brass tablet
with a Latin inscription in memory of Thomas Lawe,
an Alderman, who died in 1677, and on the south wall
are two mediæval brasses which have been removed
from the floor of the nave.

The large font is worthy of notice. It is made of
Ancaster stone and beautifully carved round the bowl.
It was designed by Pugin and presented by the Rt. Hon.
A. J. Beresford Hope, M.P., in 1853. The hexagonal
pulpit, of dark oak, is a fine specimen of carving of the
time of Queen Elizabeth. The Litany Desk was presented in 1893, and is a memorial to one John Brown.
The Lectern, formerly in the shape of a sloping desk,
but recast in 1891 to resemble an eagle, is in memory
of the Rev. Richard Conington, who died in 1861.

The chancel is reached from the nave by two steps.
The screen, which originally separated the chancel and
the nave, was illegally removed in 1590, though the
rood and statues had been destroyed before that date.
The two blocked doorways, which formerly opened on
to the rood, and also the sockets to which the chains
supporting the rood were attached, may still be seen.
About a century later another screen of classical design
was placed here, but at the restoration in 1851–3 it was

removed and now adorns the Roman Catholic Church in Boston.

The original ceiling of the chancel was panelled and had beautifully carved mouldings. This was replaced in 1781 by one much lower, which was restored and painted in 1906.

The east window of the chancel has seven lights, and was fitted with stained glass in 1853, designed by O'Connor. The subject represents the descent of our Lord from Jesse, and commences at the base of the central light with the figure of Jesse. From him spring two branches enclosing the figures of King David on the right and S. Joseph on the left, and above is the Blessed Virgin Mary holding the Infant Saviour to whom the Eastern Kings are offering their gifts. Immediately above is depicted the Crucifixion; and on either side are two Evangelists; while above this is the figure of our Lord seated in majesty with two Angels on each side in an attitude of adoration. In the other four lights are represented the Apostles, and in the tracery are figures of the Archangels Michael, Gabriel, and Raphael, and a choir of Angels with musical instruments. There is much to be admired in the design of this window, which includes reproductions of ancient works of art taken from Lincoln Minster, Gedney Church and Pinchbeck Church. The colour, however, is not good, and at present much of the window is hidden by the lofty reredos.

The sixty-two stalls, with their misericorde seats, form one of the most interesting collections in the kingdom, and are arranged in two rows on each side as far as the north and south doors in the chancel. Some of the ancient ones have been preserved, but the canopies of the upper stalls, which are a copy of those in Lincoln Cathedral, were added between 1858 and 1860. Each of these contains a niche for a statue, and the names of the donors or persons they commemorate are inscribed on brass plates. The small seats move on a hinge, and underneath are carvings in bold relief, some representing ancient legends of the saints, others events in local history, others animals and birds, or the deeds and characteristics of individuals.

East of the stalls are a north and a south door, between which, before the Reformation, was a screen dividing the chancel into two parts, forming 'Our Lady's Quere' and 'S. Peter's Quere.' In 1558, the Corporation records state that it was ordered that 'the Aldermen shall sit with the Mayor in Our Lady's quire and the common council in S. Peter's quire on the north side thereof. None of the House to talk in the church, to the ill example of others.'

The organ occupies a small chamber on the north of the chancel and is fitted with a case to harmonize with the stalls. The music and singing have from early times been an attractive part of the services in the church. The organ is first mentioned in 1480, and Leland highly commended it after his visit in 1530, when he said that the church was 'served so with such singging and that of cunning men as no paroche is in al England.' Since music was disliked by Puritans the organ was removed in 1590, and the services were conducted without music for some time. Later, however, another instrument was obtained, for records show that in 1717 another screen was erected and a gallery for singers was built near the organ. These were neglected and allowed to fall into a bad state of repair, but later in 1820 the organ was rebuilt at a cost of £850, and at the restoration in 1852 it was again enlarged and repaired for £311, and placed in its present position. Again in 1871 it was completely reconstructed and now contains three manuals, forty-eight stops, and 2,378 pipes.

The altar rails, which are made of brass and iron, are approached by ascending five more steps. They were erected in 1754 close round the altar, but removed to their present position in 1853, leaving a wide altar space. This leads to three more steps, then a foot pace to the altar, which is further raised on another step, making a total of eleven steps from the nave. The floor of the chancel is paved with Yorkshire stone, the altar space with blue and buff tiles, and the steps are cut from Devonshire marble.

Over the north and south doors in the chancel are oak canopies, and oak panelling extends from these along both walls to the reredos. In each panel as far as the altar rails is a brass plate, those on the south side being memorials to Edward Chapman Hackford (1884), Thomas Scrivener (1876), and Judith his wife (1886), John Oldrid (1849), and the Rev. John Henry Oldrid, M.A., Lecturer (1898). Those on the north are memorials of William Simonds (1817), Thomas Wells Thorpe (1887), James Edward Ridlington (1892) and Mary his wife (1877).

On the south above the panelling will be seen a tablet of alabaster representing the Resurrection, and a brass in memory of John Conington; and on the north wall a memorial in white marble executed by Chantry, the famous sculptor, to James Hollway, who died in 1882. Two very fine brasses may be seen here on the floor near the altar: one, beautifully ornamented with figures of the Apostles under canopies, has for its central figure John Strensall, Rector, clad in a cope and stole, who died in 1408. The other represents Walter Peascod and his wife, the date being 1398. On the north wall of the Sanctuary is another brass mounted in black marble in memory of John Palmer Hollway and his wife (1843).

The two oak chairs on the south side of the altar date from 1853, and the five canopied seats beyond, which resemble the stalls, contain brass plates as memorials to H. K. Bonney, D.D., Archdeacon of Lincoln, 1854; Rev. Henry Butler Pacey, D.D., 1863; John Furniss Ogle, M.A., Vicar, 1850; John Kaye, Bishop of Lincoln; and G. B. Blenkin, Vicar, 1891.

The large massive altar of English oak was consecrated in 1853, and is provided with frontals, one of these was designed by Sir G. G. Scott, and worked by the Sisters of Bethany, Lloyd Square, 1853.

The reredos was designed by W. S. Weatherley, F.S.A., and was erected in 1891 as a memorial to Walter Scrivener. Then, after more additions, it was again dedicated in 1914 as a memorial to John Oldrid, and Martha, his wife. It is thirty-two feet high and forms a screen across the chancel five feet from the east wall. It is executed in wood and much resembles those of Winchester and S. Alban's Cathedrals. A representation of the Crucifixion, with S. Mary and S. John, forms the central part, while the whole structure comprises fifty-three figures, or groups of figures, representing saints and members of the holy Catholic Church.

CHAPTER VI

OTHER OBJECTS OF INTEREST IN AND AROUND BOSTON

APART from the Church there still remain other buildings of historic and architectural interest in and around Boston for one to see.

Boston is a very compact little town, exceedingly healthy, clean and well lighted, having a business quarter furnished with attractive modern shops and residential quarters well laid out and pleasing to look upon. A glance at a plan of the town will show that it is mostly built on the east side of the river. The main thoroughfare runs nearly north and south, with the market place—a spacious irregular opening—about midway, and other streets diverging from it. The Market Place is perhaps the principal place of business, but other busy shopping centres will also be found in Strait Bargate, Wide Bargate, High Street, South Street, and West Street.

Like many old towns, Boston was early protected against its enemies by a wall and moat, though the surrounding district of creeks and fens also formed a natural protection. A few traces of the old wall which ran along the north-east side of the river may still be found, and the moat, through which the Barditch drain is now conducted, leaves the Witham near the Grand Sluice. The plan will also show the position of the gates which gave admission to the town, for they are still preserved in the names of Bargate, where Strait

Bargate opens into Wide Bargate and marks the site of the east gate; S. John's Gate, near the upper ferry, named after the Knights of S. John, and giving entrance from the south; and the west gate opening on to the bridge, which in those days spanned the river a little further down than the present bridge. Wormgate, too, was formerly the Witham Gate.

Within these limits many associations of old Boston may still be traced. Some remain as crumbled ruins and testify to its former greatness; others exist only in name, their sites being now occupied by new centres of interest.

At the entrance to the Church Close will be noticed the statue of Herbert Ingram, Esq., of Swineshead Abbey, who was a local celebrity. Herbert Ingram was born in Boston in the year 1811, and after serving in a local publisher's office, he gained further experience in Nottingham and London, and there afterwards founded the *Illustrated London News*, the pioneer of that type of paper. In 1856 he represented the town in Parliament, and again in 1857 and 1859, but in 1860 he was drowned with his eldest son while crossing Lake Michigan on the steamer *Lady Elgin*. His body was brought back to Boston for burial, but that of his son was never recovered. In 1884 his eldest surviving son was elected member for Boston, and in 1893 was created a baronet.

On the north side of the Church Close will be seen the Sessions House. This is an imposing stone structure in the Italian style of architecture, and was erected in 1841–3 on the site of the Augustine Priory. The Petty Sessions are held here each Wednesday, and the Quarter Sessions at regular intervals. Since Boston does not possess a gaol, all male prisoners are despatched to His Majesty's Prison at Lincoln, and females to Nottingham.

The Vicarage, which is a modern building, is also on

the north side of the Church; and quite near, at the corner of Wormgate, is the old Church House; ancient indeed, but very well preserved. Before the Reformation charities were dispensed here, but in 1578, it was converted into a 'House of Correction,' and in 1582 it became the residence of the Grammar School Master. At the present time it is again used as a centre for the distribution of relief, this time, by the Board of Guardians. The history of this house is interesting, for it shows that it formed part of the grant of Philip and Mary to the Corporation. It then appears to have been sold to Mr. Ingram, and later sold again by his son to the Rev. R. T. Heygate, a vicar of Boston; but it was eventually paid for by local subscriptions, and passed into the hands of trustees to be used in the interests of the Church.

In Church Street is the site of the house of John Fox, the author of the well-known *Book of Martyrs*, but it is now occupied by the Rum Puncheon. Fox was born in Boston in 1517 in the house which afterwards became the Bell Inn, but was replaced in the eighteenth century by the present building. His biographer states that Fox was brought up by his stepfather as a decided Papist, but during his undergraduate days at Brasenose College, Oxford, his views changed under the influence of his tutor, and he became a Puritan. Then, after taking his B.D. Degree in 1538 he transferred to Magdalen College, where he became a fellow; but two years later, being charged with heresy, he resigned his fellowship, and until the death of Henry VIII he lived in daily fear of persecution. During the reign of Edward VI, however, he was ordained by Bishop Ridley, and later engaged as tutor to the children of the Earl of Surrey, but when Queen Mary ascended the throne, Fox had to start on his travels again. This time he found refuge with other Reformers at Basle, and while there he began to collect information for his *Book of Martyrs*. After the death of Mary he returned to England, and was received by the Duke of Norfolk, the son of the Earl of Surrey. He was then made prebendary of Skipton in Salisbury Cathedral, but his biography shows that the last fifteen years of his life were spent in Grub Street as a writer, and he died in 1587.

The Assembly Rooms will be seen bordering on the Market Place. The illuminated clock in the centre formerly stood over the old Butter Cross in the Market Place, but this structure was removed when the Assembly Rooms were built in 1822. This is a spacious building. The large rooms are frequently used for entertainments and public meetings, and the basements serve as covered markets for butter and poultry. In the vestibule are three brass cannon of the time of Charles I, which were brought here from King's Lynn during the Civil War for the defence of the town in those troubled times.

Shodfriars Hall, on the opposite side of the Market Place, is a very interesting building of brick with heavily timbered front, and dates from 1500. Its overhanging upper story, with oak beams and plastered spaces of curious design, presents a very quaint appearance. Its history seems somewhat obscure, though there is good reason to think it may have belonged to the Dominican Friars, and later, it was probably the mansion of the Tooley family who once lived in this part of the town. In 1874 it was restored at the cost of £9,000, but the well preserved fittings inside are very curious and quite worth inspection. Part of it is now used by the Shodfriars' Social Club, and the large hall is furnished as a theatre.

A little further along South Street is Spain Lane, in which may be seen a few fragments of the Dominican Friary, which was founded in Boston by the Tilney family and occupied the site facing the Packhorse Quay. It has been suggested that these old buildings in Spain Lane may have been the southern side of the Cloister Court of the Friary. At the present time they form part of merchants' storehouses, and other remains of the Friary have been incorporated in the interior of the Clubhouse on Packhorse Quay. Spain Lane probably takes its name from the famous old family de Spagne, which flourished in Boston in the fourteenth and fifteenth centuries. Various relics have been found here; the memorial slab of Wisselus de Smalenburg, a merchant of 1340, now inlaid in the floor of the Church, was taken from the wall of a house in this street, though originally it was unearthed on the site of the Grey Friars near the Grammar School.

In South Street, too, is the famous old Guildhall, which contains relics and has associations of special interest to visitors from America, but a detailed description of this ancient structure is given in Chapter VII.

Formerly the Bedesmen's houses adjoined this Hall. Though these have been demolished, the name is still preserved in the Court known as Bedesmen's Lane, which separates the Hall from the fine old Queen Anne mansion called Fydell House.

At the bottom of South Square is the entrance to the Grammar School, a red brick building on a stone foundation, which dates from 1562. This school is one of considerable reputation, but for further details see Chapter VIII.

Behind the school fields, near S. John's Gate, are the interesting ruins of an old mansion which was formerly occupied by Lord Hussey. All that remains to-day are a square brick tower which stands in an enclosure, many traces of foundations, and an ancient wall. The history of this isolated structure, called Hussey Tower, shows that it originally formed the keep of the extensive Hall which was probably pulled down in 1780. The gate house appears to have been taken down in 1565 when the remaining part of the residence was repaired by the Corporation, and later, in 1702, the brew house and mill were ordered to be sold and removed. In 1728 the lead and timber were taken from the tower for the use of the Corporation, and some years later it was proposed to use it as a gaol, but this being unpracticable, in 1792 the enclosure, containing the tower, was exchanged for other lands with Mr. Fydell. The tower and all rights, however, were retained by the Corporation, but Mr. Fydell undertook to keep it as an ancient monument. The Husseys were a distinguished old Lincolnshire family, the last of whom was Sir John Hussey who became a Baron in 1505, but was eventually beheaded for heresy while Lord Lieutenant of the County, for supporting the Pilgrimage of Grace. His descendants in the male line, however, soon became extinct, and then the possessions of the family were sold to the Corporation by Henry VIII and are now held by Mr. Rowley.

Further on, by the upper ferry, is S. John's Gate, which formerly gave access to the town from the south. It takes its name from the Knights of that Order who had their church just outside the wall on the road which leads to Skirbeck, and also occupied the land still known as S. John's Churchyard. The remains of the church were removed in 1625, but the disused burial ground still retains old gravestones with very quaint epitaphs.

The Order also possessed a hospital which was dedicated
to S. Leonard and provided for twelve poor folk, and this
is still in existence in the form of Almshouses, which
overlook the Maud Foster Drain on the Horncastle road.

On the right of S. John's Gate is the Boston Hospital
which occupies the site of the old Steelyard. It appears
to have been started in 1871 as a Cottage Hospital, but
the present building was erected in 1874, with the
addition of a new wing in 1887 and further extensions
in 1897 and 1921. It is very pleasantly situated on the
bank of the river Witham and its extensive grounds
adjoin the Public Park.

The People's Park was obtained in 1872 and, with its
flowery borders and avenues of trees leading down to
the Witham, its bowling green, and its tennis courts, it
provides for the needs of those who desire a pleasant
retreat or active recreation. Quite near is the entrance
to the Gardens and Corporation Baths, which were
built in 1879 and are supplied with sea water.

The Docks may be approached by following the bend
in the river. As stated in a former chapter, the Port of
Boston reached the height of its fame in the thirteenth
century, but owing to the religious changes, industrial
developments, and new discoveries, its trade then
declined, though it always maintained a share of Con-
tinental commerce. At the beginning of the last century,
the business of the port was checked again by the
accumulation of silt on the bed of the river which
seriously impeded navigation. In 1885, however, the
river channel was deepened, the docks constructed, and
further improvements were made in 1900. From then
until the outbreak of the Great War a considerable
trade with the Continent was carried on, for Boston is
the natural gateway between the industrial centres and

TATTERSHALL CASTLE

the Continent. In 1914 the flourishing fishing industry also ceased, but since the war this has revived, and the trade at the port continues to increase. Ships of large tonnage now have access to the quays at Spring tides, and docks are provided with railway sidings, sheds for storing corn, machinery worked by hydraulic and electric power, and all other modern facilities for rapidly removing cargoes.

The Grand Sluice, which is quite near here, was the outcome of much drainage controversy, and was constructed in 1765 for the improvement of navigation and for regulating the drainage waters. The Lock was opened in 1883, and now that the Channel to the Deeps has been buoyed, the Port of Boston is considered one of the safest in this country.

Skirbeck Church, dedicated to S. Nicholas, is situated on the river bank not far beyond the docks and about one mile from Boston. The church dates from about 1180, and though much mutilated, is of considerable beauty. It consisted originally of the Norman chancel, early English nave, aisles of six bays erected in the thirteenth century, and the perpendicular tower which was added in 1450. Owing to its position, this church has been much damaged by the high tides and floods during the ages; and in 1571 much of the masonry was destroyed. In 1598 an attempt was made to restore the ruins, when the fine Norman chancel was removed and the present unworthy chancel was formed out of two bays of the nave. Many other structural alterations were made so that the church was then greatly reduced in size and stripped of much of its original decorations and beauty. In 1876–7 extensive repairs and constructive works were carried out, and in 1905 a further restoration was made, when portions of the church were rebuilt

I

following its original design. An interesting feature is to be found in the circular clerestory windows resembling those in Southwell Cathedral, and their position above the pillars instead of over the bays is unusual. The clustered columns of the east end arcade, with detached shafts and capitals, are also of unusual richness and beauty. There is also much to be admired in the Elizabethan pulpit, and other furnishings of the church.

The tidal river Witham, with its constant ebb and flow, is spanned by a neat and spacious bridge, from which may be obtained a delightful view of the church and its reflection in the swiftly moving waters. The present steel girder structure—leading from the Market Place to the High Street—dates from 1913, when it was erected on the site of Rennie's cast-iron bridge opened in 1807; but old records show that the Witham was crossed by a bridge at Boston from very early times. It is first mentioned in 1305 in a petition of John de Brittany, Earl of Richmond, for pontage to be granted to him for repairing the bridge at S. Botolph's; and later, we see that tolls were levied on saleable articles passing over the bridge. Such tolls as the following were exacted: $\frac{1}{2}$d. for every ten sheep, 1d. per dozen salt salmon, 2d. per sack of wool, $\frac{1}{4}$d. per qr. of wheat, $\frac{1}{2}$d. per dozen catskins, 1d. for each horse valued above 40s., and $\frac{1}{2}$d. per horse below that value, and $\frac{1}{2}$d. each for oxen and cows. The position of this bridge is not quite clear, but it may have been a wooden bridge over the position of the great sluice built by Alan de Croun in 1142. In 1312 the sluice appears to have been in a sad state of ruin, and the whole district was consequently in danger of flood. In 1500 an iron bridge was built over the sluice by Mahave Hall, the famous Flemish engineer, and was kept in repair by the Countess of Richmond until 1550, when it appears that the Corporation spent £48 16s. on its repair. In 1553 a grant was made by Queen Mary to the Corporation to support the bridge, 'which needed daily reparation.' Later, gates were constructed over the bridge for the collection of tolls for its upkeep, but in 1662 it was in 'great decay,' and as the Church of S. John was being taken down at that time, some of the materials were used in building a new bridge in 1631. Again in 1642 and in 1742 the bridge was in a ruinous state and extensive repairs were necessary; in 1807 a new iron bridge was erected a little south of the old one at a cost of £22,000, and in 1913 this was replaced by the present structure.

Much of the business of the Corporation is now conducted from the Municipal Buildings in West Street, which are of modern construction though built in the Renaissance style, in 1904 at a cost of £20,000. They comprise a fine Council Chamber and the usual Corporation offices, a Free Public Library, School of Art, and Fire Brigade Station. The building also contains various town relics and maces dating from 1683.

Bits of old Boston may still be seen in some of the narrow streets, in the quaint little cottage in Archer Lane, and in the remains of the Peascod Hall in Mitre Lane. The Red Lion Hotel, too, has a history of its own, for it originally belonged to the Guild of S. Mary and appears in the Guild records of 1515 as 'The Hospitium of the Red Lion in Bargate'; but from 1586–90 it was licensed by the Corporation 'for the sale of beer brewed out of the Borough.' The Falcon Hotel, too, was an inn of great importance before and during the sixteenth century, and in 1617 it was bought by the Corporation to be used as a granary. The Peacock and the White Hart were important posting houses in the eighteenth century.

There are now various places of amusement in this town. The New Theatre, which is part of the old Corn Exchange, was opened in 1928 ; various entertainments are also held in Shodfriars Hall, while the Scala Cinema in the Market Place is a popular picture house with a café. It appears that a theatre did not exist in Boston before 1777, though in 1567 a play was acted in the Grammar School by the School and Wates from Cambridge. Then in 1578 we read that it was ordained that there should be 'no plaies or interludes in the Church, nor Chancel, nor Hall, nor Schole House,' but later, this was cancelled for in 1579 it was agreed that the Play of the Passion of Christ should be acted in the Hall yearly at Easter and on Whitsunday. Sometime afterwards a local company of comedians performed in other large buildings, and in 1777 a theatre was built by the Corporation to accommodate 1,079 persons, though this seems to have declined in 1819 and was removed in 1850.

The Town's War Memorial, erected on Bargate Green, was designed by W. S. Weatherly, F.R.I.B.A., and unveiled by the Earl of Yarborough in 1921. The memorial consists of a massive stone base mounted on a platform of four steps, on which is raised an octagonal monolith shaft surmounted by a cross, giving a total height of twenty-eight feet. The panels bear a commemorative inscription, texts, and the names of those who gave their lives in the Great War. Quite near the memorial may be seen a British tank and a German field gun, both relics of the Great War, and also two Russian cannon, presented to the town by the War Office at the close of the Crimean War.

CHAPTER VII

THE GUILDHALL

PERHAPS, next to the Church, the most interesting relic of old Boston, and one which holds special interest for Americans, is the ancient Guildhall. It is situated in South Street and is about five minutes' walk from the Church.

The building is an ancient structure in the Gothic style, and dates from 1450. Originally it was the Hall of the Guild of S. Mary, which was the wealthiest and most important of the fifteen town guilds. The guild itself was founded in 1260 by Boston merchants, and was the great mercantile guild; but it also maintained strict religious observances, and supported the Chapel of S. Mary in the Church. In 1393 the Guild was incorporated, and probably as a result of this, the Hall was built in the next century.

At the Reformation, however, came also the surrender of the guilds, and their possessions then came into the hands of Lord Parr, Marquis of Northampton. He, apparently, did not hold them long, for soon afterwards he paid the penalty for high treason at the Tower, and his goods were forfeited to the Crown. The Corporation then saw an opportunity for their recovery, and the Guildhall passed to them as trustees by grant from Philip and Mary.

As this building was then the property of the town, in 1583 the hall and kitchens were converted into a prison, and the inner chamber into a council house, which served as an assembly room for the Council till 1835. The Quarter Sessions, however, continued to be held here till 1843, and the hall was also used for various business and social meetings. In 1909 the building again passed into new hands. This time it was purchased from the Governors of the Grammar School— the Charity Trustees—by Frank Harrison, Esq., J.P.; and he transferred it to the Corporation for their use in perpetuity. Then, by the advice of the Society for the Preservation of Ancient Buildings, it underwent necessary repairs, and though its public use is now restricted, it is open to visitors for inspection.

It will be seen that it is a fine red brick building with stone facings. During the ages much of the original structure has been demolished and other parts have been modernized; but in the west end which faces the street, there still exists a large window with perpendicular tracery, containing some remains of very ancient glass, and figures of the Apostles. The niche in the centre, with a carved canopy, formerly held the figure of our Lady, the patron saint of the guild.

The entrance is by the door below the window and admits the visitor to a low, dimly-lighted hall which has a wide staircase at the end. Beyond this hall are the kitchens, which still retain their huge fireplaces fitted with large spits and quaint smokejacks, all of which are in working order. On this floor, too, may be seen the famous Guildhall cells, and a winding staircase which leads through a trap door to the Court Room above. It was in these cells that the Pilgrim Fathers were imprisoned, for this Hall at that time served as the Borough Gaol.

If the visitor then ascends the wide staircase, he will see on the landing a large engraving of Boston Harbour,

U.S.A., and on turning to the left, the old banqueting hall. This is lighted by the perpendicular window, and has an open roof and wainscoted walls, but the room has been sadly spoilt by modern repairs. At the east end is the 'Minstrels' gallery, which is approached by a small and winding staircase. In the old days, this hall must have been the scene of many civic feasts, and was, no doubt, well served from those kitchen jacks on the floor below. On the west wall is the mace stand of Samuel Abbot, 1727, and on the north wall is a tablet in memory of Bro. Joseph Cooke, a former Mayor of Boston, 1902–3, a generous subscriber to the preservation of this ancient building.

To the right of the landing, is a small ante-chamber which once served as the Justices' Court. In the autumn of 1607 this room was the scene of the trial of the Pilgrim Fathers after their capture in Boston port on their first attempt to leave the country without legal permission. Many of the Pilgrim Fathers had come from the North Midlands, and were bound for Holland, but being betrayed by their Dutch captain they were held in custody in the Guildhall cells. It was not until 1876 that this ceased to be used as a court room, when it was repaired and the end partition was added.

The old iron-plated chest seen in this room formerly held the treasures of the Corporation, and the various other objects exhibited here are memorials of local interest. On the walls are the Borough Arms carved in wood, boards showing a list of mayors of Boston since 1545, a mace stand of William Fydell, 1729, and a tablet in memory of Capt. Meaburn Staniland, Town Clerk, who was killed in the Great War.

Beyond this room is another large wainscoted hall which also was repaired in 1722, when sash windows

replaced the original ones. In this room may be seen
an enlarged photograph of the old State House, Boston,
Massachusetts, built in 1713, but now occupied by the
Bostonian Society, and a list of members of this society
who generously subscribed to the restoration of this
Guildhall is also exhibited here. Two pictures here are
interesting: one is a valuable painting of Sir Joseph
Banks, Bart., President of the Royal Society and Recorder
of Boston, 1809–20, by the artist Phillips; and the other,
entitled 'The Painter's Wife and Daughters,' is by the
late Sam G. Enderby, a native of Boston, 1860–1921.

Over the fireplace is a brass tablet inscribed with a
summary of the last events in the history of the Guildhall.
This states that it was purchased by Frank Harrison,
Esq., J.P., from the Governors of the Boston Grammar
School—the Charity Trustees—and that by the generosity
of the inhabitants, and of the liberal donors of the
Bostonian Society, Boston, U.S.A., it was conveyed to
the Mayor, Aldermen and Burgesses of the Borough,
and was to be preserved as a memorial to the late King
Edward VII.

CHAPTER VIII

THE GRAMMAR SCHOOL

LIKE many of our ancient towns and cities, Boston had in early days an established centre of learning, the Grammar School, a very efficient and up-to-date institution to-day, yet with a foundation and a history going back to past ages.

The building, of red brick and stone, is situated at the end of South Street, and possesses several interesting features. When tracing its history we find that the school was a settled institution in the early part of the fourteenth century, for in 1329, an entry in the Lincoln Chapter Acts' Book states that the Dean and Chapter of Lincoln appointed Robert of Maston as Master. Though records do not exist before that date, there is good reason to believe that it was an endowed school from at least 1260, and owing to the antiquity and importance of the town, it may have existed even earlier. Again in 1387 the Grammar School of S. Botolph's is mentioned, when the Subdean and Chapter promised the vacancy to Mr. John of Newbald, M.A. Apparently he was appointed, but his experience here must have been short, for six months later the headship of the school was conferred on Mr. John Bracebrygge. Then in 1367–8 the 'Magister Scolarum Boston' appears among the distinguished members of the Guild of Corpus Christi; for at this time the school was situated in Wormgate, and being supported by various guilds of Boston, was one of the most famed in the country.

At the Dissolution of the Guilds in 1547, the school appears to have been suppressed, for the endowments, with other possessions of the guilds, were confiscated. These, however, in 1552 passed from the hands of the King to Lord Parr, Marquis of Northampton, but he was soon relieved of them, for being convicted of high treason at the Tower the next year, his property was forfeited to the Crown. The following year, however, many of these endowments were restored by the Charter of Philip and Mary, one of the articles of which charged the Corporation with the maintenance of the School.

Bound by this responsibility, the Corporation decided to provide a new site and buildings, so the present school was built during the year 1567–8 on part of the Mart Yard, known as Hallgarth, at the cost of £195 0s. 11d. During the erection of the new building instruction was carried on in the old school, which was afterwards sold, and the schoolmaster's house was used for the Laughton School.

This old Elizabethan schoolroom is still preserved, though, of course, many extensions and improvements have been made to meet the requirements of modern education. The east side of the old building has five windows, each with stone mullions, and labels and coats of arms blazoned on the glass. There are four similar ones on the west side, and also a large projecting bay in the centre. The north gable has a square-headed window, and immediately below is an interesting stone panel carved with the Borough Arms, and bearing the following Latin inscription:

'Ao 1567 Reginæ Elizabethæ nono, Maior et Burgenses Bostoniæ, uno et eodem consensu puerorum institutionis gratia in piis litteris hanc ædificaverunt scholam Gulielmo Gannocke Stapulæ Mercatore et tunc Maiore existenti.'

The interior is panelled in oak, and has an open timbered roof. The north window, with five lights, contains modern stained glass, representing noted Elizabethan personages: Burleigh, Drake, Shakespeare, Bacon, and Queen Elizabeth. The southernmost of the east windows is fitted with ancient glass, but each of the other windows is a memorial to some trustee or person connected with the school. The northerly one of these is in memory of Thomas Collis, John Holliday Thomas, and Thomas Wise; the next of John Hobson, Thomas Smalley Cooke, and John Oldrid; the third of Frederick Cooke, Joseph Wren, and John Carruthers Little; and the fourth of Stephen Lewin, Frederick Lyon Hopkins, and Thomas Garfit.

Many structural improvements have been made during the past century. The house for the master was built in 1828; in 1850 a lobby and classroom were added to the north end, and in 1856 another classroom was attached to the south end. More extensions were made in 1903 by the erection of science laboratories. With more recent additions during 1925–8 the original sites of the Hallgarth, Manor House, and Franciscan Friary have been enclosed, and what is virtually a new school has been erected at the cost of £25,000.

Until the eighteenth century the building was surrounded by shops, and the Hallgarth had been the scene of the great annual Fair for centuries. The school is now enclosed by a wall with iron gates. Over these is a fine piece of Flemish wrought iron work bearing the Borough Arms, which was removed from the screen in the west end of S. Botolph's Church in 1851.

The school has been under the care of several distinguished headmasters, and many notable scholars have been turned out by this old Foundation. In 1567 the

Corporation appointed their first master, Walter Wood-ruffs, and also decided that the income from certain lands should be used for providing an usher in addition to the master—and that the usher should give religious instruction. The school then had a regular succession of masters and ushers until 1752, when it appears to have declined, but in 1803 it had revived, for the prospectus shows that it had then developed into a boarding as well as a day school. In 1820 Dr. Homes was given the appointment. He had formerly been a master at Rugby, and at first proved eminently successful, but apparently he stayed too long, for in 1847 the school had so dwindled away that we are told 'there were no boys at all.' However, under the new headmaster, G. E. Patterden, B.D., in 1850, it made great progress, and by 1877 the numbers had increased to 111 day boys, 25 boarders, 4 assistant masters, and the headmaster. At the present time the school consists of over 200 boys, who are under the care of the headmaster and thirteen assistant masters.

In 1854 the school was placed under the management of specially appointed trustees, but in 1903, when the roll numbered 200 boys, a new scheme for the appointment of trustees was granted by the Board of Education. This distinguished them from Charity Trustees, for though the total endowments amount to about £1,100, the school is also dependent on grants from the Education Committee of the Holland County Council and the Board of Education. Recently the bulk of the Governors' real estate has been sold, the proceeds invested in Government securities; and the school is now administered under a scheme of the Board of Education drafted in 1922.

CHAPTER IX

TATTERSHALL

A Brief History and Description of its Church
and Castle

THE little town of Tattershall, situated on the
river Bain, about eleven miles north-east of Boston,
has a claim to be mentioned in any account of
Boston and the district around. This town, now small
and decayed, has a history, and is famed for its castle
and church. The market cross also testifies to its former
importance, and still stands, though the market is no
longer held.

The castle is a distinctive feature in the landscape of
this flat country, and may be seen for many miles around.
The original castle was built in 1240, but of this only
the outer moat and some earthworks remain. The
existing castle was built by Ralph Lord Cromwell, who
was Lord Treasurer to Henry VI from 1433–43, and
this represents the keep of that of earlier days. Originally
the castle was a strong fortress, but the present structure
consists solely of a large square tower, 117 feet in height,
and is one of the finest examples of mediæval brickwork
to be seen in England. The massive walls of local
red brick are 16 feet thick in places, and cover a base
area of 89 feet by 67 feet. At the angles rise four
octangular turrets, and four stairs lead to the central
rooms, with small chambers opening from them; but
a stairway of 181 steps leads to the south-east turret,

where there is all round a covered projecting embattled gallery resting on massive corbelled masonry. From this turret one may obtain a wide view over the Fenlands. The castle is surrounded by an inner moat crossed by a timbered drawbridge, though the outer moat has also recently been excavated. The windows and battlements are of Ancaster stone and inside may be seen on each floor the beautiful heraldic chimney pieces which are the finest in all England. In 1911 these were removed by an American millionaire who was on the point of sending them to the United States. The late Earl Curzon of Kedleston, however, intervened, and bought the Castle, which he afterwards presented to the nation. The work of repair, occupying over two years, was carried out under the direction of Mr. Weir, architect for the Society for the Preservation of Ancient Buildings, and the Castle was formally reopened in August, 1914.

The Guard House is now converted into a museum containing an interesting collection of prints, paintings, and pottery, but the Castle itself now provides a unique example of the castellated architecture of the fifteenth century.

There is, however, very little history connected with Tattershall. It suffered much damage in the great Civil War, and it was the only fortified place in the county which was garrisoned by the Parliament in 1648. The last resident in the Castle appears to have been a pensioner, who occupied the gallery in the southern wall, his purpose there being to fire a beacon in case of invasion.

The Church of Holy Trinity is a spacious perpendicular edifice built by Ralph, Lord Cromwell. Though it was unfinished at his death in 1455, it was completed by one of his executors, William of Waynflete, Bishop of Winchester, and founder of Magdalen College, Oxford. It is a noble cruciform building with a massive west tower with four pinnacles, chancel, nave with six bays, aisles, north porch, and lofty transepts; and was built as a Collegiate Church when a College was founded here in 1438.

The chancel retains three sedilia, a piscina, and an aumbry, and there are also piscinæ in both transepts.

The interesting stone screen dividing the chancel from the transepts, was erected by Robert de Whalley, who was a member of the College, in 1528, and who is buried beneath its archway. It has two recesses for altars, with pillared piscinæ on its west front, and on the east side is a curious projection with two stone book rests.

In the north transept will be seen some very fine brasses commemorating the founder and two of his nieces, and other brasses of three members of the College: William Moore, Provost 1456, William Sympson, Chaplain 1519, and Provost Warde 1500–20. In Haines' *Book of Monumental Brasses*, published in 1861, mention is made of seven memorial brasses then existing in this church. Under the canopies are memorials of Joan (Stanhope), Lady Cromwell, 1479, and Maud, Lady Willoughby d'Eresby, 1497.

The lower part of the east window contains good remains of old glass, but much of the beautiful glass from Tattershall representing the Apostles and Saints, together with many shields and arms of Cromwell, now adorn the Church of S. Martin, Stamford.

The College of Holy Trinity, Tattershall, was founded in 1439 by Ralph, Lord Cromwell, then the Treasurer of the Realm. It consisted of a Provost, six priests, six laymen, and six choristers, but the College was dissolved in 1545. The almshouses for thirteen poor people were also of Cromwell's foundation, and were placed under the care of the same Warden. They are situated near the churchyard, and still exist for the use of ten poor persons.

HOLY TRINITY CHURCH, TATTERSHALL

CHAPTER X

CROYLAND

A Brief History and Description of its Abbey and Bridge

'And they rowed away for Croyland——
Into the air, as they rowed on, whirred up the great
skeins of wild fowl innumerable, with a cry as of all the
bells of Croyland.'

C. Kingsley.

NO one having come to the Fenlands should depart
without a visit to the little town of Croyland,
celebrated for the ruins of its beautiful Abbey
and its curious Triangular Bridge. The history of this
Abbey, interwoven with that of Croyland itself, takes us
back to the early days of Christianity in England, when
our country was an Island of Saints.

Croyland stands isolated in the midst of the Fens,
twenty miles south-east of Boston, twelve miles from
Peterborough, and four and a half from Postland, its
nearest railway station. On all sides it overlooks one
vast expanse of low flat country.

In the old days, the site of Croyland appears to have
been a desolate oozy island, surrounded by swamps and
meres abounding in fish and wild fowl; but in recent
years, by effective drainage, this dreary region has been
transformed into highly productive cornlands.

As one makes one's way along the straight roads over
this low, level plain, with the Abbey in sight in the
distance, one naturally wonders why such a noble building

should have been erected in this inaccessible wilderness of bygone days. History tells us that this famous Abbey of the Benedictine Order was founded in 714 by Ethelbald, King of Mercia, in honour of S. Guthlac, the Patron Saint of the Fens, for the story of the life of this Saint was written by Felix, an old Saxon Chronicler, and monk of Croyland.

S. Guthlac, we are told, was the son of a Mercian nobleman and was born in 673. In his early years, he appears to have been the leader of a band of youths who spent their lives in fighting and plunder, in accordance with the wild barbarism of that period; but at the age of 24 years, S. Guthlac suddenly reformed, and surrendering his home and paternal wealth, sought refuge in the Abbey at Repton, Yorkshire. Here he stayed for two years; but craving for solitude and a more austere life, he left the monastery and went in search of a lonely island in the marshes. Then, under the guidance of Tatwine, a boatman, he decided to land where the boat should first be stranded; and on S. Bartholomew's Day, 699, this anchorite arrived with his servant named Beccelm, on the desolate island of Croyland.

The site of his landing and cell, a quarter of a mile east of the Abbey, is still known as the Anchorite, or Anchor Church Hill; and the ruins remained there until 1720. Here S. Guthlac lived a life of prayer and devotion; and the wild birds of the island became his friends, and rested in the thatch of his lonely cell. Soon, however, his solitude was broken by the numbers who sought his advice and direction, among whom was the fugitive king, Ethelbald of Mercia. But on Wednesday in Passion Week, 714, he died, and two years later, on S. Bartholomew's Day, 716, Ethelbald laid the foun-

CROYLAND ABBEY

dation stone of the Abbey, which was to perpetuate the memory of this great Saint, and to be a thankoffering for the help and advice he had received from him. At the same time he endowed it with the island of Croyland and other lands along the river Welland.

Unfortunately this monastic house of Ethelbald's foundation did not stand long, for we read that, during the Danish invasion of 870, most religious houses in this part of England were destroyed, Croyland among them. The work of restoration, however, was soon begun, and under the care of Abbot Thurkteyl, a stone Saxon structure replaced the former Abbey of wattle and thatch. Very little is known of this building, for it, too, met a similar fate, and perished by fire in 1091, when its famous library of three hundred MSS. was also destroyed. Rebuilding, however, was commenced immediately by Abbot Ingulphus; but the work of the third Abbey, a great Norman structure, was undertaken by his successor, Abbot Joffrid of Orleans. Under his direction, a most extensive church and buildings were erected, for records show that the work was begun in 1113 when '28 foundation stones were laid, and a dinner given to 5,000 people.' This solid Norman church, with its north and south transepts, central tower, and choir measuring ninety feet in length, was also seriously damaged, first by the earthquake of 1118, and again by the fire of 1145.

Though portions of this third Abbey may still be seen, the remains to-day, however, are chiefly those of the fourth Abbey, which was really a work of reconstruction, since much of the old material was reshaped and erected in the perpendicular style between the years 1392 and 1469, under the Abbots Overton, Upton, and Lytlyngton.

Before the Reformation, extensive grounds had been

covered by these fine monastic buildings, for old plans show that this Church, when perfect, consisted of a nave of nine bays, with aisles 186 feet long and 87 feet wide; the transepts of two bays each having also east and west aisles; the choir of five bays, 90 feet in length; the central tower; the north-west tower; and a western porch. Beyond the east end of the choir was a detached bell tower which had been erected in 1255. The cloisters, 95 feet square, adjoined the south transept, and with their vaulted alleys, 12 feet in width, connected by two doors into the Church.

Reports show, however, that the monastery was frequently involved in expensive lawsuits owing to raids on its cattle and goods; and in 1344 it became so much impoverished that the Abbot was unable to meet his creditors, and the Abbey received special protection from Edward III. Nevertheless, in spite of serious damage to property and heavy costs of lawsuits, the monastic life of Croyland maintained a widespread fame for courtesy and hospitality, for we read that 'Courteous Croyland' afforded refuge for kings, nobles, and poor alike, and provided a sanctuary for strangers as well as for friends. At the same time the monks were the great movers in all works of improvement in the country around, and they so drained and cultivated the land, that we are told the Abbot 'had the increase of an hundred fold of what seed soever he sowed'; and the monastery became so enriched by these plentiful crops, 'that the whole country thereabouts was supplied therewith.'

This old monastery, too, was the nursery of religion and education through all the times of bitter persecutions, and a haven of refuge to all in distress; for an old chronicler has said, 'It might not unworthily have been called the very castle of the Gospel.' Although little of its ancient glory is left to it, Croyland still lives on, for it is the parent of Magdalene College, Cambridge, which was founded by this monastery under Abbot Lytlyngton.

At the Dissolution of the Monasteries, in 1539, this old and wealthy foundation was surrendered and soon stripped of all its treasures and beauty. It then became subject to the violence and outrage of the Commissioners of Henry VIII, who at once tore down the ornaments, demolished the choir, transepts, and central tower, leaving a scene of utter destruction and desolation.

> 'No mattins at midnight;
> Book and chalice quite gone;
> Pluck away the leads
> Over their heads;
> And sell away their bells
> And all that they have else.'
>
> SKELTON.

Among this heap of wreckage was left standing the western arch, the nave, and aisles, to be formed into a church for the use of the town. These were preserved, and a wall with a square window filled up the east end. The roof of the nave was vaulted in wood, and that of each aisle in stone. Further misfortune, however, was to befall the Abbey, for in 1643, it was bombarded by the army of Oliver Cromwell, and brought to destruction. Then the many years of isolation and lack of care which followed, reduced this ancient building to a pile of ruins. In 1720 the roof of the nave collapsed and was never restored; and in 1743 the south aisle was taken down to provide buttresses for the north side of the tower. The north side of the nave, however, remains, and is very carefully preserved, since it has always served as the Parish Church.

THE PRESENT REMAINS

A walk round the relics of this venerable foundation will show that the extensive monastic buildings and cloisters were on the south side of the great Church, but it is now almost impossible to trace their position. Among the present remains will be seen the central portion of the magnificent west front, revealing three stages of architecture. The lowest portion is early English and includes a recessed doorway and a fine series of old statues under enriched canopies dating from 1171. These are arranged in four tiers and represent Apostles, Saints, Patrons, and Benefactors, among whom are S. Bartholomew, S. Guthlac, and King Ethelbald. The quatrefoil over the doorway is interesting, as illustrating in carved medallions, five scenes taken from the life of S. Guthlac. One represents the arrival of the Saint at Croyland, where the only inhabitants of the island were a sow and her young family; and the centre one shows the Saint compelling Satan to bring stone for the Abbey. The upper portion of this front was rebuilt in the fourteenth century as an imitation of the front of Wells Cathedral.

The west tower, built by Abbot Upton in 1427, still exists, and from its plain parapet rises the sixteenth-century, dwarf octagonal spire. The ruined nave, now all open to the sky, the remains of the tower at the east end of the grand Norman arch, and the stone screen, all testify to the Abbey's former importance. Since the floor of this lordly nave has recently been excavated by the removal of three feet of the accumulation of centuries, the nave can now be seen in its true proportions, and

the grandeur of the beautiful Norman arch which
formed the western arch of the central tower of the old
Abbey of Abbot Joffrid's construction, can again be
fully appreciated.

Among the ruins, fragments of the work of Abbot
Joffrid may still be seen in a part of the west end of the
south aisle, exhibiting four tiers of varied arcading, the
two western buttresses of the nave, and the western
arch of the central tower, enriched with zigzag moulding.

During recent years various works of reconstruction
have been carried out. In 1860 the west front was
restored under the direction of Sir Gilbert Scott, and in
1888–9, 1898, and 1904, other extensive repairs were
done by the late Rector, T. H. Le Boeuf, who was
responsible for the erection of a new chancel to the
present Church and for preserving the Abbey from
complete ruin.

As one enters the Church, which, it will be remembered, was part of the north aisle of the Abbey, one will
pass through the fine vaulted porch, over which is a
room for the priest known as the Parvise. This room,
the east window of which overlooks the High Altar, is
now furnished as a Chapel, and is approached by a
stairway just inside the Abbey. On the right of the
doorway will be seen a Cell, or 'Canarie Chapel,' in
which those claiming sanctuary at the Abbey were
received; and on the left was the mortuary which is
now occupied by the stairway. The open tower presents
fine proportions and its four galleries have recently been
brought into use for the ringers and choir. Here, on
the south wall, is a stone lid of a casket which was used
for Heart burial; and inserted in the north-east pier may
be seen the Norman Immersion Font of Abbot Joffrid's
time, which has a capacity for twenty-five gallons of

water. The separate font belongs to the perpendicular period. The chief glory of the Church, however, lies in the beautifully vaulted roof with its six bosses. The groining springs from pillars which the builders of the perpendicular period formed from the columns of the Norman pillars. This work is very unusual, but the effect is really beautiful and graceful.

The three westernmost bays on the north side open into three Chapels, dedicated to S. Katharine, S. John the Baptist, and the Holy Trinity. The middle one is used as a Chapel, but for the present the other two serve as vestries.

The interior has numerous mural tablets, some of which are quite ancient, but well preserved, and the old plans and drawings of the monastery exhibited, are very interesting.

According to old records, the Abbey was formerly rich in stained glass, and the few fragments which remain, have been preserved in the top tracery of the large south window. The beautiful chancel screen is highly valued, since it was rescued from the general wreckage at the Dissolution. It formerly enclosed the Lady Chapel in the north transept, and is the work of Simon Eresby, a brother of the monastery in 1413.

Before leaving the Abbey one's attention may be arrested by the Abbey bells. Recently, they have broadcast their cheery message by wireless throughout the length and breadth of England, and who knows how much farther yet? But it is to the native of the Fens alone that they whisper their secret; for their voices are part and parcel of his heritage through the ages. From the dim past of Saxon Eadgar's reign, when a certain pious Abbot 'Cast six bells,' their voices have called to the hearts of the Fenmen. Abbot Thurkteyl, who lived a century before the Norman Conquest, recorded his delight in them; and his successor, fired by his enthusiasm, no doubt, deemed them worthy of a fitting sanctuary, and built the first bell tower for the first real peal of bells in England! For upwards of 800 years, daily has come the curfew call to 'cover the fires'; and that call will probably continue 800 years and more. One of the bells, whose voice is heard to-day, was heard first in the days of Queen Elizabeth. And to-day, as in the days of the old monks of Croyland, those bells take part in the life of the dweller in the Fens. They drive home to him daily the passing of time, for the Curfew bell daily gives him the day of the month. The Shriving Bell of Shrove Tuesday still bids him solemnly prepare to meet his God. He knows the voice of each bell as it rings out its message of joy or of pain. One tells of the passing of a little child; another the safe ingathering of an aged saint. No day passes but they voice for him in some way the mysteries of time, of life, of death, and eternity. Could he but once give utterance to what these things mean, it would be 'with a cry as of all the bells of Croyland.'

THE TRIANGULAR BRIDGE

Croyland is justly proud of its famous old Abbey, but this isolated little town also claims another attraction in its curious Triangular Bridge. This quaint old structure should not be overlooked, for it is the greatest curiosity of its kind in the country.

It stands in the centre of the town, about three minutes' walk from the Abbey. Formerly it spanned the river Welland, which divided into two streams at this point. One branch followed a circuitous course past the Abbey, and on to join the river Nene, while the other flowed on to Spalding. At that time the bridge provided three roads over these two streams, leading to Peterborough, Stamford, and Spalding, respectively. Each of the three roads of the bridge is supported by a separate arch, and the three arches meet at the centre, where formerly stood a large cross. The architecture is peculiar and interesting, for it will be noticed that it consists of three arched piers, forming a triangular base and meeting overhead to form one groined arch, so that really there are not three bridges, but one bridge, hence it is sometimes called the Trinity Bridge.

The history of this bridge is interesting, for the present structure dates from the fourteenth century; but it appears to have replaced a former bridge referred to in the Charter of Eadred in 943, which, though constructed of wood, was similar in form. The width of the bridge —only eight feet—and the steepness of the roads, show that it was never intended for drawn vehicles, but in its construction, consideration must have been given to navigation, since we read that Edward IV embarked from here when leaving the Abbey for Fotheringhay Castle.

Water still flows under the bridge, but it is not visible, for it flows in covered channels under the ground.

In the old days the Cross on the bridge marked a station for pilgrims visiting the shrine of S. Guthlac, and on each Good Friday, the bridge still does duty in an old and sacred custom, when a service is held here by the Rector of Croyland and the Abbey choir.

A crowned statue stands on the south side of the bridge. Various suggestions have been made as to its representation, but as it originally occupied a position on the west front of the Abbey, and was transferred to the bridge during the alterations in 1720, it is now

THE TRIANGULAR BRIDGE, CROYLAND

generally believed to represent the figure of our Saviour with a loaf of bread in His hand.

To the Croyland people, the bridge is a much valued relic of their town's past importance, and provides for them a congenial meeting point at the present time.

S. BOTOLPH, STATUE ON TOWER